SpringerBriefs in Economics

Development Bank of Japan Research Series

This series is characterized by the close academic cohesion of financial economics, environmental economics, and accounting, which are the three major fields of research of the Research Institute of Capital Formation (RICF) at the Development Bank of Japan (DBJ). Readers can acquaint themselves with how a financial intermediary efficiently restructuring firms in financial distress can contribute to economic development.

The aforementioned three research fields are closely connected with one another in the following ways. DBJ has already developed several corporation-rating methods, including the environmental rating by which DBJ decides whether or not to make concessions to the candidate firm. To evaluate the relevance of this rating, research, which deploys not only financial economics but also environmental economics, is necessary.

The accounting section intensively studies the structure of IFRS and Integrated Reporting to predict their effects on Japanese corporate governance. Although the discipline of accounting is usually isolated from financial economics, structural and reliable prediction is never achieved without sufficient and integrated knowledge in both fields.

Finally, the environmental economics section is linked to the accounting section in the following manner. To establish green accounting (environmental accounting), it is indispensable to explore what the crucial factors for the preservation of environment (e.g., emission control) are. RICF is well equipped to address the acute necessity for discourse among researchers who belong to these three different fields.

Titles in the series are authored not only by researchers at RICF but also by collaborating and contributing researchers from universities and institutions throughout Japan. Each proposal is carefully evaluated by the series editor and editorial board members, who submit written reports that appraise each proposal in terms of academic value and rigor and also provide constructive comments for further improvement. At times, the editorial board appoints external referees to provide additional comments. All prospective authors also presents their research findings to the editorial board in face-to-face editorial board meetings, where the series editor and editorial board members provide further detailed comments on the findings, methodology, overall presentation, and advice in preparing the book manuscript in English.

More information about this subseries at http://www.springer.com/series/13542

Tadanori Yosano · Takayoshi Nakaoka

Utilization of Soft Information on Bank Performance

The Roles of Relationship Lending in Competitive Local Markets

DBJ

Springer

Tadanori Yosano
Kobe University
Kobe, Hyogo, Japan

Research Institute of Capital Formation
Development Bank of Japan
Chiyoda-ku, Tokyo, Japan

Takayoshi Nakaoka
Kindai University
Osaka, Japan

Research Institute of Capital Formation
Development Bank of Japan
Chiyoda-ku, Tokyo, Japan

ISSN 2191-5504 ISSN 2191-5512 (electronic)
SpringerBriefs in Economics
ISSN 2367-0967 ISSN 2367-0975 (electronic)
Development Bank of Japan Research Series
ISBN 978-981-13-8471-4 ISBN 978-981-13-8472-1 (eBook)
https://doi.org/10.1007/978-981-13-8472-1

This Springer imprint is published by the registered company Springer Nature Singapore Pte Ltd.
The registered company address is: 152 Beach Road, #21-01/04 Gateway East, Singapore 189721, Singapore

Preface

This book explores the effects of soft information utilization in the decision process for lenders, especially concerning small and medium-sized enterprises (SMEs) in regional markets. This study is one of the first studies that use questionnaire survey data from lender representatives, analyzes the relationship between the financial metrics of a lender's performance and soft information factors, and further applies this analysis to interbank completion. The authors' empirical results suggest that utilizing soft information allows lenders to attain a more precise lending decision.

The Financial Services Agency in Japan introduced an action program in 2003 that requires regional banks to shift from transaction-based lending to relationship lending. Against that background, this book examines the influence of relationship lending on a lender's performance. This study found that relationship lending allows lenders to charge a higher premium to counteract the high risk involved with SMEs. This book also examines how relationship lending affects lending performance in interbank competition. The conclusion is that, even though interbank competition has negative effects, a bank in a competitive local market can acquire an informational advantage to limit its own loss.

This book specifically conducts a factor analysis using the survey questionnaire data to categorize questionnaire items into three soft information factors: organizational systems, networks or alliances/partnerships, and business and management leadership. The authors' findings suggest that information production, especially network and business/leadership information, plays an essential role in promoting a bank's profitability. These effects are strong even when banks face high interbank competition. Relationship lending not only improves bankers' lending techniques, but also encourages intimate personal interactions and further fosters and enhances their community knowledge—which enable them to survive in a highly competitive market.

These findings will be useful to scholars and policymakers in the field of relationship lending, especially against the backdrop of advances in intelligent information technologies.

Kobe, Japan Tadanori Yosano
Osaka, Japan Takayoshi Nakaoka

Acknowledgements

We would like to thank Kamon Iwatsubo, Nobuyoshi Yamori, Kazuo Ogawa, Yoshiaki Ogura, Hirofumi Uchida, Hans Degryse, and Steven Ongena for their helpful comments. We are also grateful to the participants of 2010 Barcelona Banking Summer School, 5th Applied Econometrics Conference at Osaka University, and 2010 FMA meeting and, particularly, Klaus Schaeck, Gregory F. Udell, and Allen N. Berger. We appreciate their valuable comments and suggestions. Any errors are our own. This research was financially supported by a grant-in-aid from the Zengin Foundation for Studies on Economics and Finance.

Contents

About the Authors

Tadanori Yosano is Associate Professor at the Graduate School of Business Administration at Kobe University, and Visiting Scholar of the Research Institute of Capital Formation, Development Bank of Japan. His fields of interest in research are within accounting for intangibles, intellectual capital reporting, accounting for M&A, accounting for employee stock options as well as soft information role in the bank–firm relationship. He received a bachelor's degree in economics at Kyoto University in 1994 and a Ph.D. in business administration at Kobe University in 2002. His major publications include: Outperforming markets: IC and the long-term performance of Japanese IPOs (with C. Nielson, G. Rimmel). *Accounting Forum* (2015); Analysts' perceptions of intellectual capital information (with S. Sakakibara, B. Hansson, H. Kozumi). *Australian Accounting Review* (2010).

Takayoshi Nakaoka is working at Kindai University in Japan as Associate Professor and gives lectures on statistics and econometrics. His current research focuses on relationship banking, corporate cash holding, and information management in the organization. He received a Ph.D. in commerce at Kobe University in 2011 and worked as Researcher at SMBC Nikko Securities Inc. His major articles (in Japanese) include: The determinants of debt structure in Japan. *Osaka Bankers Association Forum Paper Series* (2016); Corporate cash holdings: cross country analysis after the Financial Crisis of 2007 (with N. Isagawa). *Kokumin Keizai Zasshi* (2014).

Chapter 1
Introduction

Abstract This chapter highlights the significance of relationship lending in lenders' decision-making process, especially concerning small and medium-sized enterprises (SMEs) in Japanese regional markets. Generally, relationship lending has been a common practice in credit financing for financial institutions of all sizes; it is in contrast to the term "main bank," which is specifically used to describe the close bank–firm relationship for large firms in Japan. Although the main bank relationship has tended toward decline, relationship lending has particularly gained attention not only due to the Japanese Financial Services Agency introducing its 2003 action program, but also due to rather close ties between regional banks and SMEs owing to these small businesses' opacity. Contemporary literature suggest that the firm-bank relationship produces an invaluable asset when it is long lasting by using proxies for relationship lending. Meanwhile, this article uses a questionnaire survey to identify the components of the information used in relationship lending. Further, it investigates soft information factors' influence on a lender's performance, specifically in a competitive local market. Therefore, this chapter summarizes the characteristics of soft information, and the role and functions of these pieces of information in the lending decision process.

Keywords Relationship lending · Main bank · Action program · Soft information · Business assessment · Hard information · Transaction lending

1.1 The Bank–Firm Relationship in Japan

This work examines relationship lending's effectiveness and significance in lenders' decision-making process, especially as it concerns small and medium-sized enterprises (SMEs) in Japanese regional markets. Relationship lending is a financial institution's provision of financial services based on a long-term investment in firm- or borrower-specific information. Such information is obtained through intimate interactions between the financial intermediary and the firm or borrower. Specifically, after Berger and Udell (2002) introduced this concept in academic research, relationship lending has been subsequently characterized as the accumulation and utiliza-

T. Yosano and T. Nakaoka, *Utilization of Soft Information on Bank Performance*, Development Bank of Japan Research Series,
https://doi.org/10.1007/978-981-13-8472-1_1

tion of "soft" information in the lending decision. Further, Berger and Udell (2002) argued that producing soft information—defined as unquantifiable, unverifiable, and sometimes subjective—is an essential part of relationship lending. Therefore, soft information is innately subject to intense difficulties when faced with the client firm's external boundaries. The inaccessibility of soft information impedes a rival financial intermediary from intervening in the lender–borrower relationship. Moreover, the inaccessibility of soft information creates insurmountable barriers against the competitive institutions that protect the revenue opportunities resulting from investments.

While soft information is utilized in the lender's loan screening and monitoring processes, the former process is specifically emphasized. This is because the process enables lenders to assess potential customers' creditworthiness, and attract and secure them as loyal clientele, a process directly connected to the lender's market strength and success. The barriers created by soft information work to insulate existing clientele from a credit assessment if a rival institution attempts to enter into its lender–borrower relationship. However, a financial institution will not rely on evidence from financial statement analyses, while the SME's opacity accelerates the difficulties in a credit analysis. In other words, opaque firms face dire judgment. In Japan, especially until the mid-1980s, firms had close ties to specific financial institutions—commonly referred to as "main banks"—that typically served as primary sources of credit. These main banks typically monitored firms' operational and investment activities through large-sum loans. Further, main banks sometimes hold a significant share of firms' equity, and even appoint a liaison officer to senior positions on their board to enhance their monitoring activities (Weinstein and Yafeh 1998, p. 636). Focusing specifically on this monitoring process is a variant of relationship lending.

The "main bank" system has specifically and thoroughly functioned as a means for city banks and some regional banks to offer commercial lending to large businesses under strict segregation rules for its clientele. This has especially been the case in the commercial lending arena since World War II. City and regional banks[1] played a primary role in providing funding resources to large businesses in accord with the Banking Act. However, shinkin banks and credit unions—which were mandatory—were expected by law to provide commercial lending to SMEs. Further, relevant regulatory legislation confined shinkin banks' and credit unions' clientele to SMEs.[2] The term "main bank" is specifically used in the close bank–firm relationship for large firms in Japan. However, relationship lending in the general sense has been a common practice in credit financing among financial institutions of all sizes. A special feature of relationship lending in Japan is the relationship's longevity. For example, a dataset provided by Uchida et al. (2008) reveals the average relationship

[1]Thirteen city banks have been affected by a wave of financial reorganization since the late 1990s. Some have declared bankruptcy and since ceased to exist, while others integrated to form five new city banks. As an amalgamation of smaller city banks, these five existing banks are large in size, and therefore, are called "mega banks."

[2]Shinkin banks are regulated by the Shinkin Bank Act, and credit unions are required to comply in accordance with both the Small and Medium-Sized Enterprise Cooperatives Act and the Act on Financial Businesses by Cooperative.

duration between a firm and its prime financing provider in Japan is 31.8 years, while a dataset from Berger et al. (2005) indicates this relationship in the United States is 8.7 years. Thus, Japan has more relationship longevity than the United States.

The Japanese financial system's drastic deregulation and liberalization—represented by the relaxation of cross-border capital transactions—has urged firms to shift from "arm's length" lending with a main bank toward bond financing in their domestic markets and in Euromarkets (Weinstein and Yafeh 1998, pp. 636–637). The sharp decline in revenue opportunities from main bank relationships has encouraged banks' "herd behavior," inefficiently following other banks' behavior without any thorough, elaborate assessment of their creditworthiness (Nakagawa and Uchida 2011, pp. 618–619). Further, the late 1980s' asset-pricing bubble accelerated this herd behavior, as soaring asset prices concealed firms' underperforming business activities as well as any deterioration of their creditworthiness. After the asset-pricing bubble burst in the early 1990s, financial institutions were saddled with non-performing loans; some were forced to declare bankruptcy, while others pursued realignments and alliances in an effort to ensure their ongoing viability.

While the main bank relationship is an intense manifestation of relationship lending and has been on the decline in Japan (Aoki and Patrick 1995), relationship lending itself has gained particular attention since Japan's Financial Services Agency (FSA) introduced a 2003 action program to enhance relationship-lending functions among small/medium-sized and regional financial institutions. This program aimed to dispose of non-performing loans from small/medium-sized and regional financial institutions, thus ensuring the revival and sustainability of financial functions for SMEs. Alternatively, the FSA has strived to normalize mega banks' problematic non-performing loans by tightening assessments of assets, enhancing capital adequacy,[3] and strengthening governance in their organizational structure (FSA 2002). Relationship lending emphasizes an income-based approach: a screening and valuation process occurs based on the company's ability to generate future cash flows before a business is loaned money. The action program anticipates small/medium-sized and regional financial institutions to evaluate the company's future cash flows using soft information, and thus, enhance and strengthen their credit risk assessment capabilities in the fiercely competitive lending market. In contrast, the main bank relationship plays a primary role in ex-post monitoring by assessing sound, proper, and appropriate affordability in short-term loans, as well as dispatching a liaison officer to the company's board of directors (Aoki and Patrick 1995).

[3]In 1993, the FSA implemented a capital adequacy ratio requirement of 8% for banks engaging in international business and 4% for others, expecting that commercial banks would maintain sufficient bank capital to reduce their insolvency risk. The measure of adequacy used is a bank's available capital as a percentage of the bank's risk-weighted credit exposure.

Although the main bank relationship has overall weakened or disappeared over the past two decades, a strong, closely knit relationship with financial institutions is still vital for SMEs, as they generally have a recorded poor credit history and opaque disclosures. The FSA initially launched its 2003 action program to reduce information asymmetry between borrowers and uninformed lenders through building stronger relationships. After this introduction, the program's aim shifted in 2005 from disposing non-performing loans financed by small/medium-sized and regional financial institutions to ensuring these financial institutions' soundness and creditworthiness—which require these financial institutions to strengthen customer relationships—while improving their profitability. An action program's top priority—the importance of business assessments in SME lending—was further introduced in a new Financial Monitoring Policy (FSA 2014). This initiated the monitoring of small and medium-sized/regional financial institutions to ensure the steady implementation of SME lending based on such business assessments.

Although the outstanding loan balance provided to SMEs from private-sector financial institutions has decreased, from 296.2 trillion yen at the end of 2000 to 227.6 trillion yen at the end of 2004, it should be noted that lending to SMEs remains important. These numbers were noticeably larger than those provided to big businesses; private-sector financial institutions' collective balance to large firms was 131.0 trillion yen at the end of 2000 and 97.5 trillion yen at the end of 2004. Further, the high ratio of small business loans to total banking assets at the end of 2002 was 74.0% and 82.0% for regional and second-tier regional banks, respectively. These were comparably higher than that of city banks at the end of 2002, which stood at 60.3%. Meanwhile, manufacturing SMEs are characterized by a heavy reliance on credit loans: the ratio of credit loans to total assets in 2002 was 31.8% on average for SMEs with total assets of less than five billion yen. This figure is 10% greater than data from the United States, in that the ratio of credit loans to total assets in 2003 was 21.8% on average for US SMEs with total assets of less than five million dollars (Japan Small Business Research Institute (JSBRI) 2005). Manufacturing SMEs exhibited outstanding balances from primary loan banks of 85 million yen, with an average loan period of five years in Japan (Nakaoka et al. 2011).

Researchers have examined the benefits of relationship lending in terms of both lenders and borrowers for the past two decades. Much of this literature before the early 2000s discussed soft information's influence on credit conditions, such as credit availability, loan interest rates, and collateral assets. Prior theoretical research specifically focused on lender performance, showing that lenders engaging in relationship lending obtained larger monopolistic rents, or higher interest rates (Sharpe 1990; Rajan 1992). However, these previous research results have presented a mixed picture across countries. Depending on the balance of transaction-based to relationship lending technologies, soft information's effects differed. Furthermore, the effects varied across borrowers' characteristics (Petersen and Rajan 1994, 1995; Berger and

Udell 1995). Further, Kysucky and Norden (2016) recently conducted a systematic review and meta-analysis of 101 studies among several countries to indicate not only that the relationship generally benefits borrower firms, but also that this may depend on the intensity of competition in lending markets and the firms' relationship status. Additionally, recent empirical studies demonstrate that both soft (qualitative) and hard (quantitative) information sets are complementary in lending decisions (Bartoli et al. 2013; Nakaoka et al. 2017). Moreover, Nakaoka et al. (2017) found that voluntary assurance in Japanese SMEs' financial statements produces value when the firm-bank relationship is long lasting.

Researchers since the early 2000s have increasingly focused on relationship lending's role in interbank competition. On one hand, Boot and Thakor's (2000) seminal paper suggested that interbank competition would accelerate lenders' engagement in relationship lending, and enable them to extract higher rents from borrowers (Malafronte et al. 2014). On the other hand, Boot and Thakor's (2000) work further indicated that borrowers obtain beneficial added value from lender-borrower relations when lenders shift from transaction-based lending toward initiating their engagement in relationship lending, but this value might be small compared to that in a monopolistic market. Furthermore, Dinc (2000) suggested that at the same time interbank competition would lower the threshold of borrowers' available credit and diminish lenders' enthusiasm toward costly commitments with borrowers. Similarly, Hauswald and Marquez (2006) suggested that interbank competition would reduce lenders' investment in information acquisition due to the anticipated decrease in interest rates.

However, the research presented in the previous paragraph is based primarily on theoretical models with scant empirical evidence to support their predictions. Moreover, almost all previous research has investigated this claim through the proxies of relationship lending: duration, or the duration of time since a lender granted the first loan to a borrower; scope, or the breadth of the relationship, measured by the number of different financial products or services a borrower receives from a lender; and the borrower-lender distance, or the physical distance from the lending office to a borrower. Previous research used proxies for relationship lending due to the difficulties inherent in numerically measuring soft information. Schwarze (2007) provides one exception by composing indicators based on questionnaires to German banks to investigate soft information's influence on loan performance.

As with Schwarze's (2007) work, this book incorporates a questionnaire survey and conducts factor analysis to identify the components of soft information that benefit lenders. The current work is one of the first to analyze the types of soft information significant to lenders, which may then be used to improve lenders' ability to judge credit risk and thus to raise profitability. It also illustrates the benefits of utilizing soft information, especially if lenders face strong interbank competition.

1.2 Enhancing Functions of Relationship Lending in Japan Since the Early 2000s

Japan's FSA introduced its action program after substantial decline in outstanding lending to SMEs until 2002[4] as well as prolonged regional economic stagnation (JSBRI 2004). This program required small and medium-sized or regional financial institutions to shift from transaction-based lending to relationship lending (FSA 2003). Essentially, the action program has a two-pronged objective: first, to revitalize SME financing, and second, to ensure small and medium-sized/regional financial institutions' soundness while improving their profitability. The action program encourages lenders to primarily judge SMEs' creditworthiness based on a business assessment—or an observation of their businesses' strengths and weaknesses—without relying on collateral assets from the SME loan market. Through this program, the lender–borrower relationship has tightened to ensure both lenders' and borrowers' soundness.

After a two-year intensive period, the action program was revised in 2005 (FSA 2005). In this setting, the Organization for Small and Medium Enterprises and Regional Innovation, Japan (SME Support, Japan), established the SME Intellectual Asset-Based Management Finance Working Group in 2007 under the SME Intellectual Asset-Based Management Forum of Experts to strengthen SME lending based on soft information. The working group conducted a questionnaire survey in 2008 to assess the use of soft information in the SME lending decision-making process (SME Support Japan 2008). This book uses this questionnaire data to categorize three soft information factors: organizational systems, networks or alliances/partnerships, and business and management leadership.

An action program's top priority issue—the importance of a business assessment in SME lending—has been reflected in the FSA's Supervision of Small/Medium-Sized and Regional Financial Institutions since its 2008 revision (FSA 2008). The FSA further introduced a new Financial Monitoring Policy (FSA 2014) and initiated the monitoring of small and medium-sized/regional financial institutions to ensure steady business assessment-based SME lending. The new Financial Monitoring Policy considers the relationship-lending concept—which encourages financial institutions to lend based on their assessment of borrowers' business prospects and not collateral—in loans to SMEs. The shift from transaction-based to relationship lending has progressed since the introduction of an action program in the early 2000s; however, according to a recent survey by the Japan Small Business Research Institute (JSBRI 2016), traditional loans dependent on collateral assets remain the mainstream form of SME lending.

It is noteworthy to examine the limitations of soft information—as well as whether using soft information is effective—to steadily put an action program's priority issue into practice through appropriate and practical measures.

---

[4]Small and medium-sized/regional financial institutions' SME lending had declined by approximately 20% during the period of 2000 through 2002 (JSBRI 2004).

1.3 Soft and Hard Information

Banks or lenders in the bank–firm relationship scrutinize businesses and their management teams to determine if they are visible borrowers. Lenders enter into credit contracts with borrowers by analyzing and assessing their qualifications for a loan through their business performance, financial conditions, and sometimes collateral assets. Additionally, lenders, when necessary, gather and process other qualitative information, such as managerial competencies, key customers' status, and employees' expertise, to assess borrowers' creditworthiness. Lenders also determine their credit contracts' terms and conditions, including their credit limit, credit period, and loan interest rates. On one hand, the former information collected through financial statements and collateral is quantitative and verifiable, and therefore designated as "hard" information. This information is easily condensed as numbers, and its content is independent of the collection process (Liberti and Petersen 2018). On the other hand, the latter, such as management leadership and key suppliers' status, is both unquantifiable and unverifiable, and often proprietary and subjective. It is gathered through personal interactions between lenders and borrowers. In contrast to hard information, this type of information is called "soft" information.

Hard information is more appropriate for lenders to process and reduce to a numeric score than soft information (Liberti and Petersen 2018), an inherent feature of which makes it extremely difficult for the lender to express numerically. When lenders manage to represent soft information in numbers, its quantification ultimately results in a substantial reduction of its content.

This book's authors have categorized soft information into three distinct groups based on survey data: organizational systems, networks or alliances/partnerships, and business and management leadership. An organizational system is the structure a business adopts to organize its functions and operations among multiple products or services. An organizational system is either based on the company's different internal functions or the different divisions according to its products or services. All of these divisions might share such general functions as human resources, accounting, and information technology. Accordingly, an organizational structure involves competency management, which provides the foundation to manage strategic talent management practices such as workforce planning, acquiring top talent, and developing employees to optimize their strengths. Industrial IT networks are also a crucial structural component. Networks or alliances/partnerships include the market relationships and cooperation established between firms, institutions, and people. Vertical networks range from suppliers and sub-contractors to the end customers, while horizontal networks span all aspects of a business, such as co-development, co-marketing, and collaborative sales. Regarding business and management leadership, the former involves organizations' principal activities, the competitive landscape, and their market positioning; the latter includes management leadership, managerial competencies, and succession planning.

Table 1.1 The categories of the sets of information in the lending decision process

Type		Information source	
		Non-exclusivity available for users?	
		Yes	No
Quantifiable without information loss?	Yes	Hard and Public	Hard and Private
	No	Soft and Public	Soft and Private

These sets of information, which are divided into two major categories—quantifiable (hard and non-quantifiable (soft)—can be further separated by information source: exclusive (private) and non-exclusive (public) information, as shown in Table 1.1. Kysucky and Norden (2016) posit that these dimensions are essential to understanding the benefits of relationship lending. In Table 1.1, four different categories can be found among these distinct types of information:

"Hard and public" information — This can be collected numerically and non-exclusively, and is available to all information users. This includes, for example, financial information compiled in financial statements as well as non-financial information gathered from other public sources, such as the number of employees or patents. This information is utilized in lending decisions.

"Hard and private" information — This is not non-exclusive, but could be represented numerically, such as personal assets owned by a company's manager.

"Soft and public" information — This contrasts hard and private information, as it cannot be collected numerically but has a non-exclusive characteristic available to all information users, such as information from newspapers or annual reports.

"Soft and private" information — This can be accumulated through a company's long, close-knit customer relationships. This information category is the most important in the context of relationship-lending research, and includes management's capabilities, internal assets and skills, human resources, and a company's technological superiority

1.4 Centralized and Decentralized Organizations

Loan officers typically request loan applicants to submit their financial statements and business plans in the lending process. Officers also sometimes require applicants to provide collateral assets, which have many forms and require an assessment or evaluation. Most commonly, collateral is real property, the value of which is primarily determined by a real property appraiser. In gathering this hard information, lenders have few business ties with borrowers. Further, hard information is easier to reduce to a figure and process, as in credit scoring models. Collected hard information is also straightforwardly transmitted within financial institutions, and can be delivered upstream or downstream in multi-level hierarchies along a formal line of reporting. Information flows through vertical communication, either between or among an organization's subordinates and superiors. Hard information can also be transmitted between divisions, departments, or units within the same organizational hierarchy.

Therefore, hard information gives large-scale lenders an advantage in processing extensive credit application data. Large-scale lenders with abundant tangible and intangible resources have a superior position to handle many loan applications. Advanced technologies also secure large-scale lenders an advantageous position in developing innovative data-processing capabilities through numerous resources. These capabilities enable lenders to conduct data-driven decision making and implement high-performance credit models. Financial institutions collect large amounts of data to generate specific scores by applying either statistical or expert techniques, which ultimately determines the client's credit risk. Large-scale lenders' ability to handle and analyze vast quantities of information enable them to realize the cost-reducing benefits and leverage economies of scale in hard-information lending.

In contrast, loan officers obtain soft information through interactions with borrowers and, for example, judge managerial competencies and validate sales projections. However, such information is difficult to document in reports to relay to their superiors (Stein 2002). Therefore, hierarchical organizations cannot intensely use soft information in loan assessments, as these organizations are characterized by many layers between their top management and subordinates. Subsequently, lenders who employ a horizontal structure and operate with few levels between managers and loan officers have a superior advantage against soft information lending. This horizontal structure enables lenders to minimize the leakage in information content while soft information is transmitted to the management layer.

This book's authors specifically focus on small and medium-sized/regional financial institutions with more decentralized organizational structures compared to megabanks in Japan. Similarly, Hattori et al. (2015) used Japanese survey data to find that branch managers actively collect and retain borrowers' soft information in small banks. Thus, the current work analyzes whether small and medium-sized/regional financial institutions utilize their competitive advantage against soft information lending from the perspectives of both profitability and solvency.

1.5 Small, Medium-Sized, and Large Enterprises

Large firms ordinarily have their financial statements audited pursuant to either securities or commercial laws. Moreover, they might be regarded as highly aware of the economic accountability to their stakeholders, and therefore, their financial statements and business plans are considered to have relatively high standards of trustworthiness. Hard information provides an overwhelming advantage in terms of loans to large corporations, while soft information is certainly necessary to validate corporations' potential growth and solvency.

Alternatively, SMEs prepare annual financial statements and submit them to tax offices according to the Income Tax Act and Tax Administration Act. However, auditors typically do not review or audit their financial statements. Additionally, managerial accountability and firm responsiveness[5] are not well-developed, in that their financial statements and business plans are both informational yet opaque (Berger and Udell 2002). Lenders who receive loan applications from SMEs must evaluate the relevance and reliability of applicants' financial conditions and assess their business plans' workability and credibility by gathering the aforementioned soft information. Thus, soft information plays a critical role when lending to SMEs.

The gathering and processing of soft information requires loan officers' expertise and labor. It also requires repetitive personal interactions and a subsequent intimate relationship with borrowers. This strengthens the lender–borrower relationship and enables lenders to gain specific knowledge of SMEs' businesses and judge their overall health. Therefore, smaller banks have a relative advantage in loaning to SMEs due to the proximity and personal relationships between both parties. In actuality, smaller banks in both the United States and Japan allocate large percentages of their loans to smaller firms, and vice versa (Berger et al. 1995, 2001; Berger and Udell 1996; Uchida et al. 2008).

This book investigates the influence of loans to SMEs as well as the borrower's proximity to the lender. Based on the latter, it can be inferred that the borrower is geographically closer to the lender when the lender has more branches in a regional area.

1.6 Lending Technologies for SMEs: Transactional and Relationship Lending

Lending technologies generally fall into two categories: transaction-based ("arms-length") lending, and relationship lending. The former primarily gathers and processes hard information, represented by financial statements and collateral assets, to subsequently evaluate the prospects of repayment. To assess the borrower's ability to repay the loan, the loan officer carefully studies the borrower's financial state-

[5]Firm responsiveness is the degree to which a firm is willing to provide a thoughtful response to stakeholders and commit to continue working on the issue (Bundy et al. 2013).

ments, and assesses hard assets as collateral if needed, as hard information used to screen borrowers and hard assets as collateral can be cost effective (Beck et al. 2018). Financial statement lending is transaction-based, in that a borrower's sound financial statements provide confidence in its expected future cash flows as a primary source of repayment. Large firms' financial statements are audited and transparent, and therefore, provide financial stability. Additionally, the financial statements of SMEs with long histories may also be highly reliable, and subsequently, those firms are suitable for financial statement lending.[6]

Another type of transaction-based lending is asset-based lending, in which the loan or line of credit is secured by inventory, accounts receivable, and/or balance sheet assets.[7] Fixed asset lending is also transaction-based (Berger and Udell 2006), in which a term loan is based on such fixed assets as equipment, motor vehicles, and real estate. It can be used to acquire additional equipment and improve the client's financial stability.[8] A recent, prosperous transaction-based type of lending is credit risk modeling. Credit risk models are largely divided into two categories: the option-pricing or statistical approaches. The default event, which occurs if a borrower cannot repay a loan, is central to credit risk. The former structural credit risk model estimates the credit default rate based on the movement of a firm's enterprise value.[9] The latter credit-scoring model estimates the credit default rate based on many firms' financial figures, non-financial data, and credit history.[10] The credit-scoring model calculates firm scores with this information factored into predict the borrower's probability of default. Asset-based lending, fixed assets lending, and the credit-scoring model enable lenders to assess repayment prospects even when informative financial statements are unavailable (Frame et al. 2001).

The collecting of hard information—and processing, in some cases—can be delegated to less-skilled workers or computers. Processing and analyzing substantial amounts of stored hard information enables lenders to create new value-added information. Fewer interactions with borrowers enable distant lenders to enter into transaction-based loans.

Loan officers in relationship lending primarily gather soft information through multiple interactions with borrowers over time and/or across products and/or services

[6]Financial statement lending is generally subject to financial covenants during the period of the loan in order to protect lenders' rights.

[7]A borrower provides a lender with a security interest in their assets.

[8]As with asset-based lending, the underlying assets in fixed-asset lending are pledged to the lender as collateral. However, asset-based lending differs in its credit period, as the term loan based on fixed assets is typically a long-term contract.

[9]The option-pricing model estimates the credit default rate based on the movement of a firm's enterprise value. Therefore, this model is appropriate for listed firms with observable equity prices. It is also suitable for listed firms because of the scarce occurrence of default, which makes it difficult to apply a statistical approach.

[10]Specifically, small business credit scoring is used for term loans and lines of credit for amounts up to one million dollars; this is primarily based on personal and business credit history and other financial information. Those pieces of information are collected by financial institutions, and often from commercial credit bureaus (Berger and Udell 2006).

(Boot 2000). Loan officers also collect soft information from the local community, which involves borrowers' business relationships with counterparties and borrowers' reputations in the local industry. Gathering soft information requires much time and effort, as its collection and processing requires expert knowledge and skill pertaining to the industrial sector and region. Thus, loan officers are typically granted more authority and discretion in the lending process. Soft information often remains proprietary to loan officers because it is difficult in nature to document, verify, and transmit (Berger and Udell 2006). Such features represent the stark organizational difference between transaction-based and relationship lending, as lenders risk losing some of this precious information while it is transmitted to top management. A closer proximity between the loan officer and the management layer is appropriate to prevent the loss of soft information.

Regarding lending to SMEs, financial institutions adopt either or both of the two lending types: transaction-based lending, which specifically addresses the problems with informational opacity using hard information; and relationship lending, which is significantly based on the soft and qualitative information gathered over the course of the relationship (Berger and Udell 2006). Although large financial institutions have a competitive advantage in transaction-based lending, small and medium-sized financial institutions have delivered credit through both transaction-based and relationship lending methods.

This book specifically focuses on relationship lending according to the Japanese government's initial focus on enhancing small and medium-sized/regional financial institutions' relationship lending practices. First, this book studies whether relationship lending contributes to regional financial institutions' performance, including loans' profitability and bad loan ratios. The authors have divided soft information into three categories based on survey data: organizational systems, networks or alliances/partnerships, and business and management leadership. This book investigates what types of soft information influence lender performance, as well as whether any combination among the three types of categorized soft information significantly contributes to lender performance. Second, this book also examines how relationship lending affects lending performance in interbank competition.

1.7 Conclusions

This chapter specifically highlighted the significance of relationship lending between regional banks and SMEs in Japan. Relationship lending has been a common practice in credit financing among financial institutions of all sizes. In contrast, the main bank system—which is a notable characteristic of Japanese financial systems and an intense manifestation of relationship lending (Aoki and Patrick 1995)—has specifically and thoroughly functioned in large banks' and some regional banks' commercial lending to large businesses. The main bank system has dramatically declined after the Japanese government drastically deregulated and liberalized the financial system in the mid-1980s, as large firms' raising of capital has shifted from arm's-length lending with a main bank to bond financing. However, relationship lending has gained particular attention, specifically since the FSA introduced its 2003 action program concerning the enhancement of the relationship-lending functions among small/medium-sized and regional financial institutions. A strong, close-knit relationship specifically between regional banks and SMEs is still vital, as small businesses have recorded poor credit history and generally opaque disclosures. One prominent solution to decrease the information asymmetry between borrowers and uninformed lenders has been thought to involve the building of more strong relationships. The action program's priority issue—the importance of business assessments in SME lending—has been a central part of the lending market's financial regulations. This was further introduced in a new financial monitoring policy (FSA 2014) to ensure the steady implementation of SME lending based on business assessments within small and medium-sized/regional financial institutions.

Such business assessments anticipate that small/medium-sized and regional financial institutions will evaluate companies' future cash flows using soft information, and thus, enhance and strengthen their credit risk assessment capabilities in the competitive regional lending market. As soft information is difficult to document, verify, and transmit, loan officers can obtain soft information through their interactions with borrowers. This information is difficult to document in reports and transmit to lenders' superiors (Stein 2002), and thus, the intense use of soft information in loan assessments is suitable for lenders who employ horizontal management structures and operate with few levels between managers and loan officers. Therefore, this book specifically focuses on small and medium-sized/regional financial institutions with more decentralized organizational structures than Japan's megabanks. The following chapters will investigate relationship lending's influence on regional banks' financial performance, with a focus on loan profitability and bad loan ratios, specifically in competitive local markets. Prior to its main analyses, the next chapter in this book will provide a recent literature survey regarding soft information's role in relationship lending. The following section uses a factor analysis to categorize soft information into three factors.

1.8 Outlook

This book is organized as follows: the next chapter provides a recent literature survey regarding soft information's role in relationship lending. First, the authors illustrate how the presence of informational asymmetry in the lender–borrower relationship creates an informational borrower lock-in for the lender, and thus, the lender obtains ex post monopoly power and achieves advantageous monopolistic rents. Second, the authors demonstrate how local market competition motivates the lender to lean toward engaging in relationship lending, which could curb decreased profits due to interbank competition. Third, the authors describe how soft information stored during relationship lending enables the lender to attain a sound, quality loan portfolio. Fourth, the authors further determine how an informational advantage insulates the lender from local market competition, although this deteriorates the lender's loan portfolio quality.

Chapter 3 first introduces the Japanese banking industry and the conventional classifications of depository financial institutions in Japan. This aims to provide an understanding of Japanese regional banks, the characteristics of which constitute a sample of analyses. Second, the authors review the survey data from small and medium-sized/regional financial institutions used in the analysis. Third, the authors explain how the three types of soft information are extracted from the survey questionnaire. This chapter further presents the degree to which regional banks utilize soft information in lending-decision processes, the extent of the soft information's effect on regional banks' credit conditions, and the preliminary results of soft information's influence on lender performance based on univariate analyses.

Chapter 4 provides descriptive statistics and illustrates the influential determinants which impact lender performance other than soft information that our analyses must consider. This chapter uses multivariate analyses to determine not only what type of soft information impacts lender performance, but also whether any combination of soft information types contributes to lender performance. Further, it investigates soft information's previously mentioned potent influence on lender performance under interbank competition. This chapter further demonstrates that the estimates of the multivariate analyses' parameters are not sensitive to the exact specification used. Additional tests confirm the robustness of the multivariate analyses' empirical results.

Chapter 5 interprets the empirical results regarding soft information's influence on lender performance, specifically in competitive local markets. The authors focus on the differences in uncertainty among three latent factors: organizational systems, networks or alliances/partnerships, and business and management leadership. This illustrates how each latent factor can be used in the lending decision according to the distances between banks and their business borrowers. The uncertainty surrounding these types of soft information decreases during the period in which information on targeted borrowers is gathered and measured; each piece of information is condensed, and its role might subsequently differ across a varied spectrum from the early to late stages of the collection. This chapter then provides some concluding remarks.

References

Aoki, M., & Patrick, H. (1995). The Japanese main bank system: An introductory overview. In M. Aoki & H. Patrick (Eds.), *The Japanese main bank system: Its relevance for developing and transforming economies*. Oxford: Oxford University Press.

Bartoli, F., Ferri, G., Murro, P., & Rotondi, Z. (2013). SME financing and the choice of lending technology in Italy: Complementarity or substitutability? *Journal of Banking & Finance, 37*(12), 5476–5485.

Beck, T., Ioannidou, V., & Schäfer, L. (2018). Foreigners vs. natives: Bank lending technologies and loan pricing. *Management Science, 64*(8), 3792–3820.

Berger, A. N., Goldberg, L. G., & White, L. J. (2001). The effects of dynamic changes in bank competition on the supply of small business credit. *Review of Finance, 5*(1–2), 115–139.

Berger, A. N., Kashyap, A. K., Scalise, J. M., Gertler, M., & Friedman, B. M. (1995). The transformation of the U.S. banking industry: What a long, strange trip it's been. *Brookings Papers on Economic Activity, 1995*(2), 55–218.

Berger, A. N., Miller, N. H., Petersen, M. A., Rajan, R. G., & Stein, J. C. (2005). Does function follow organizational form? Evidence from the lending practices of large and small banks. *Journal of Financial Economics, 76*(2), 237–269.

Berger, A. N., & Udell, G. F. (1995). Relationship lending and lines of credit in small firm finance. *Journal of Business, 68*(3), 351–381.

Berger, A. N., & Udell, G. F. (1996). Universal banking and the future of small business lending. In A. Saunders & I. Walter (Eds.), *Universal banking: Financial system design reconsidered*. Chicago: Irwin Professional Pub.

Berger, A. N., & Udell, G. F. (2002). Small business credit availability and relationship lending: The importance of bank organisational structure. *The Economic Journal, 112*(477), 32–53.

Berger, A. N., & Udell, G. F. (2006). A more complete conceptual framework for SME finance. *Journal of Banking & Finance, 30*(11), 2945–2966.

Boot, A. W. (2000). Relationship banking: What do we know? *Journal of Financial Intermediation, 9*(1), 7–25.

Boot, A. W., & Thakor, A. V. (2000). Can relationship banking survive competition? *The Journal of Finance, 55*(2), 679–713.

Bundy, J., Shropshire, C., & Buchholtz, A. K. (2013). Strategic cognition and issue salience: Toward an explanation of firm responsiveness to stakeholder concerns. *Academy of Management Review, 38*(3), 352–376.

Dinc, I. S. (2000). Bank reputation, bank commitment, and the effects of competition in credit markets. *The Review of Financial Studies, 13*(3), 781–812.

Frame, W. S., Srinivasan, A., & Woosley, L. (2001). The effect of credit scoring on small-business lending. *Journal of Money, Credit and Banking, 33*(3), 813–825.

FSA. (2002). *Program for financial revival -Revival of the Japanese economy through resolving non-performing loans problems of major banks-*. Financial Services Agency. Retrieved from https://www.fsa.go.jp/news/newse/e20021030.pdf.

FSA. (2003). *Action program concerning enhancement of relationship banking functions*. Financial Services Agency. Retrieved from http://www.fsa.go.jp/news/newse/e20030328-1a.pdf.

FSA. (2005). *Background of the new action program (FY 2005 and 2006)*. Financial Services Agency. Retrieved from https://www.fsa.go.jp/en/policy/reform/20050329.pdf.

FSA. (2008). Annual supervisory policies for small- and medium-sized and regional financial institutions for program year 2008. *FSA Newsletter October 2008*. Financial Services Agency. Retrieved from https://www.fsa.go.jp/en/newsletter/2008/10a.html#tp01.

FSA. (2014). *Financial monitoring policy for 2014–2015 (Policy for supervision and inspection)*. Financial Services Agency. Retrieved from http://www.fsa.go.jp/en/news/2014/20141225-1/01.pdf.

Hattori, M., Shitani, K., & Uchida, H. (2015). The repository of soft information within bank organizations. *Journal of Money, Credit and Banking, 47*(4), 737–770.

Hauswald, R., & Marquez, R. (2006). Competition and strategic information acquisition in credit markets. *The Review of Financial Studies, 19*(3), 967–1000.

JSBRI. (2004). *White paper on small and medium enterprises in Japan: The limitless potential of the diversity of small and medium enterprises*. Japan Small Business Research Institute. Retrieved from http://www.chusho.meti.go.jp/pamflet/hakusyo/H16/download/2004hakusho_eng.pdf.

JSBRI. (2005). *White paper on small and medium enterprises in Japan: Structural change in Japanese society and the dynamism of small and medium enterprises*. Japan Small Business Research Institute. Retrieved from https://www.fsa.go.jp/en/policy/reform/20050329.pdf.

JSBRI. (2016). *White paper on small and medium enterprises in Japan: Earning power to open the future*. Japan Small Business Research Institute. Retrieved from http://www.chusho.meti.go.jp/pamflet/hakusyo/H28/PDF/2016hakusho_eng.pdf.

Kysucky, V., & Norden, L. (2016). The benefits of relationship lending in a cross-country context: A meta-analysis. *Management Science, 62*(1), 90–110.

Liberti, J. M., & Petersen, M. A. (2018). Information: Hard and soft. *Review of Corporate Finance Studies,* cfy009.

Malafronte, I., Monferrà, S., Porzio, C., & Sampagnaro, G. (2014). Competition, specialization and bank–firm interaction: what happens in credit crunch periods? *Applied Financial Economics, 24*(8), 557–571.

Nakagawa, R., & Uchida, H. (2011). Herd behaviour by Japanese banks after financial deregulation. *Economica, 78*(312), 618–636.

Nakaoka, T., Takada, T., & Uchida, H. (2017). Same information, different valuation: New evidence on the value of voluntary assurance. *Center for research on startup finance working paper series, 9*. Center for Research on Startup Finance, Graduate School of Business Administration, Kobe University.

Nakaoka, T., Uchida, H., & Yamori, Y. (2011). Relationship finance in Japan (2): Evidence from the latter part of the "Survey on Current Situation of Corporate Finance in Japan" (Rire-syonshippu gata kinyu no jittai (2): Nippon no kigyo fuainansu ni kansuru jittaichosa no kouhan bubun no gaiyou, Japanese). *Economic Science (Keizai kagaku in Japanese), 59*(2), 1–27.

Petersen, M. A., & Rajan, R. G. (1994). The benefits of lending relationships: Evidence from small business data. *The Journal of Finance, 49*(1), 3–37.

Petersen, M. A., & Rajan, R. G. (1995). The effect of credit market competition on lending relationships. *The Quarterly Journal of Economics, 110*(2), 407–443.

Rajan, R. G. (1992). Insiders and outsiders: The choice between informed and arm's-length debt. *The Journal of Finance, 47*(4), 1367–1400.

Schwarze, F. (2007). *Relationship banking and profitability—An empirical survey of German banks.* Retrieved from http://dx.doi.org/10.2139/ssrn.967235.

Sharpe, S. A. (1990). Asymmetric information, bank lending, and implicit contracts: A stylized model of customer relationships. *The Journal of Finance, 45*(4), 1069–1087.

SME Support, JAPAN (2008). *Guidelines for practices of intellectual asset-based management for small and medium enterprises*. Organization for Small & Medium Enterprises and Regional Innovation, Japan.

Stein, J. C. (2002). Information production and capital allocation: Decentralized versus hierarchical firms. *The Journal of Finance, 57*(5), 1891–1921.

Uchida, H., Udell, G. F., & Watanabe, W. (2008). Bank size and lending relationships in Japan. *Journal of the Japanese and International Economies, 22*(2), 242–267.

Weinstein, D. E., & Yafeh, Y. (1998). On the costs of a bank-centered financial system: Evidence from the changing main bank relations in Japan. *The Journal of Finance, 53*(2), 635–672.

Chapter 2
Theory and Hypotheses: The Effects of Using Soft Information on a Lender's Performance, Specifically in Interbank Competition

Abstract This chapter provides a survey of recent literature on the utilization and role of soft information in relationship lending, especially as it concerns SMEs in regional markets. Contemporary literature suggests that a complex relationship exists between using soft information and lender performance, although some empirical evidence supports soft information's positive effect on loan profitability, and convincingly argues that such information effectively functions under greater interbank competition. This chapter summarizes recent theoretical and empirical advancements in literature, and consequently develops hypotheses regarding how such information might prove advantageous to financial institutions in both normal conditions and with interbank competition. First, a highly marginalized lending market creates monopoly rents allowing lenders that strategically collect and use soft information to achieve better lending performance. Second, lenders in competitive local markets can acquire an informational advantage to limit their own losses through relationship lending, although interbank competition negatively affects loan performance. Chapter 4 then tests the authors' proposed arguments.

Keywords Relationship lending · Soft information · Regional market · Regional banks · Interbank competition · Loan profitability · Bad loan ratio

2.1 Informational Asymmetry and Lock-In

Many SMEs face difficulty in raising external funding and struggle with financial constraints; further, their financial structure sharply contrasts with that of large enterprises. First, SMEs have a low equity ratio at 27.3%, but a high ratio of short/long-term borrowing, or 40.7% in 2005.[1] On one hand, their financing is more inclined to rely on borrowing, and thus is strongly affected by banks' lending attitudes and specific circumstances. On the other hand, large enterprises' 2005 equity ratio (36.1%) was greater than what they had borrowed (23.5%; Uehara 2007). This particular

[1] Source: Ministry of Finance Japan (2005), *Financial statements statistics of corporations by industry, annually*.

T. Yosano and T. Nakaoka, *Utilization of Soft Information on Bank Performance*, Development Bank of Japan Research Series,
https://doi.org/10.1007/978-981-13-8472-1_2

situation can occur due to the fact that informational opacity might result in poor credit assessments and high default rates. Therefore, less accurate information hinders SMEs' access to external funds, such as corporate bonds and equities. This constraint for SMEs is also characterized as a result of a market failure or credit rationing (Stiglitz and Weiss 1981; Storey 2016; Vos et al. 2007). Another obvious cause is that lenders do not experience economies of scale in SME lending, as quantities of lending—no matter how small—should require the same screening and assessment costs as well as administrative expenses; therefore, lenders favor lending to large enterprises. Lenders offering loan to SMEs tend to provide loans secured by collateral assets, such as real estate, to compensate for the various risks SMEs face and any challenges in their obscure business prospects and circumstances. However, SMEs sometimes fail to provide sufficient collateral assets to lenders. Therefore, SMEs ordinarily face financial constraints, and have no choice but to procure funds, not only to enhance their working capital, but also to facilitate capital investments from financial intermediaries.

At its most fundamental, the lender's role is to provide funds to informationally opaque SMEs under severe financial constraints arising from informational asymmetries. The lender obtains the necessary information, such as what the SMEs' owners and local markets gained over time through lender–borrower relationships, in order to fulfill loan requests from SMEs. Informational opacity precludes borrowers' access to public capital markets, and thus, local lenders search for borrowers with a geographic proximity that allows them to observe and accumulate the soft information necessary to assess these borrowers' creditworthiness (De Young et al. 2008). Therefore, banks' important role in this instance should resolve the problems in providing external sources to informationally opaque SMEs (Berger et al. 2001), while information asymmetries simultaneously create substantial profit-making opportunities for local lenders. Lenders first screen prospective borrowers through relationship services (Diamond 1991), in which the possibility of retracting credit exerts enough subtle pressure to persuade borrowers to conduct their investments and other business activities with integrity (Stiglitz and Weiss 1983). Consequently, lenders can monitor borrowers and control their decisions. Second, incumbent lenders can exploit an informational advantage over their competitors. In the process of lending to an informationally opaque firm, the lending banks acquire advantageous firm-specific information over non-lenders. As the lender–borrower relationship intensifies and information asymmetries increase between lenders and non-lenders, the latter face an adverse selection problem that deters non-lenders from entering into lending relationships. Subsequently, borrowers face high costs in switching lenders (Schenone 2010). Third, as a consequence of past lending, incumbent lenders have accumulated borrowers' private, qualitative information—albeit imperfect—regarding their probabilities of repayment (Greenbaum et al. 1989). Given such circumstances, incumbent lenders can create information barriers to non-lenders, paving the way for lenders to keep their clients away from potentially competitive rival lenders; this can lead borrowers to lock themselves in an entrenched lender–borrower nexus. This also enables lenders to create ex-post monopoly power and charge high interest rates to informationally captured borrowers, which ordinarily face financial constraints and have difficulties in finding external sources other than lending.

Such forms of the intimate lender–borrower relationship could allow lenders to obtain the necessary information to conclude appropriately customized loan agreements, thereby securing profitability. In fact, SME lending through relationship development and non-standardized procedures provides lenders with revenue-generating opportunities. Carter et al. (2004) and Carter and McNulty (2005) reported that small lenders have an information advantage in evaluating credit to small businesses, as these smaller lenders can make better choices from available small business loans and earn a higher interest rate for more customized service than that with large lenders.[2]

Obtaining soft information still enables incumbent lenders to block non-lenders to enter into the relationship-lending segment, even though technologies may advance and other available information—such as collected statistics on the client's detailed transactional history with one or more external sources as well as their loan payments—could partially substitute for an intimate relationship. The soft information obtained and accumulated through long-term, repetitive, and personal relationships with borrowers have specific characteristics; it is difficult to quantify, verify, and document, and thus tends to impede other potential competitors. It also restricts access to opaque borrowers, and therefore provides a certain level of exclusivity to allow lenders the advantageous benefit of monopoly rents from the secured lender–borrower relationship. As a lender–borrower relationship intensifies, soft information is increasingly accumulated, and competitors face high informational barriers. Consequently, soft information solidifies an incumbent lender's position, which leads to the following hypothesis:

Hypothesis 2.1 *The highly marginalized lending market creates monopoly rents, allowing lenders that strategically collect and use soft information to achieve higher lending performance.*

Scarce empirical research has examined the influence of using soft information on lender performance, although Carter et al. (2004) and Carter and McNulty (2005) found relationship lending positively affects lender performance. These authors posited that the small business lending market is characterized by the use of soft information and relationship development. Schwarze (2007) investigated the influence of qualitative information on loan performance through questionnaires to German banks. He constructed qualitative indicators, such as customer relationships and internal ratings, and then found that such indicators positively impact loan performance.[3]

Contrary to Hypothesis 2.1, Greenbaum et al. (1989) point to the possible entry of competitors with relatively lower interest rates. Their strategies intend to recover ini-

[2]Carter et al. (2004) and Carter and McNulty (2005) compared the differences in business loan yields between small and large banks in the U.S. banking industry by controlling for market concentration, costs of funds, and a variety of other factors that might influence yields from 1993 to 2001.

[3]Schwarze (2007) used two alternative loan performance measures: the return on equity and the operational margin, the latter of which equals $1 - (\text{administration effort} + \text{loan losses})/\text{operational income}$.

tial losses from future monopoly rents by establishing a more stable lender–borrower nexus. They argue that continuing the option-like lender–borrower relationship—the longevity of which enhances the borrower's information quality and consequently reduces the variance in the lender's return from lending—diminishes the option value. Lenders indeed exploit monopolistic power and charge high interest rates to long-standing borrowers, but this simultaneously increases the borrower's likelihood of switching banks, and thereby decreases the relationship's expected duration. External competitors can observe the lender–borrower relationship's longevity and thus can more easily offer loan contracts to those borrowers, as an observable relationship signals that those parties are highly trustworthy. As a result of this type of situation, the borrower's departure enlarges the incumbent lenders' need to search for applicants at lower, more favorable interest rates, which causes expected losses coupled with applicant searching costs that might also offset previous borrowers' monopoly rents.

Scarce empirical evidence supports relationship lending's negative influence on lender performance, as Ergungor (2005) reported that relationship lending in the period from 1992 to 2002 did not add any value for lenders, using small business loans as a proxy for relationship lending. The article especially focused on community banks to reveal that even small community banks that are more aggressive in small business lending exhibit weak profitability in relationship lending.[4]

2.2 Interbank Competition, the Shift to Relationship Lending, and Relationship Lending's Effect on Profitability

One established market structure-performance relationship is that market concentration positively affects loan profitability, which is supported by empirical evidence from numerous studies. Berger and Hannan (1989) studied 470 banks in 195 local US markets with quarterly observations over a two and a half-year period. Their work indicated that a high concentration allows lenders to exercise collusion or other forms of noncompetitive behavior, which result in less favorable interest rates for borrowers and higher profits to lenders.

This book primarily aims to determine whether interbank competition influences lenders' behavior regarding relationship-based lending, and hence, their loan profitability. Petersen and Rajan (1995) present a simple model that highlights the distinction between concentrated and competitive credit markets, and investigate the

[4]"Community banks" in the United States are typically defined as those with total assets of less than $1 billion. However, Ergungor (2005) singled out a "small community bank" category that consists of banks with total assets of less than $150 million. These banks are often obligated to make small business loans because they cannot devote more than 10% of their capital to any single borrower. Thus, banks with total assets between $150 million and $1 billion and those with assets greater than $1 billion will be called "large community banks" and "large banks," respectively (Ergungor 2005).

loan amounts that lenders finance as exclusive relationship lenders. Their model revealed that interbank competition constrains both lenders' and borrowers' credit availability. Lenders in monopolistic credit markets can backload interest payments when firms are young or in financial distress—which serve as a sort of subsidy—and extract rents later. This monopoly power enables lenders to construct intertemporal revenue opportunities, which consist of minimum revenues (close to zero), or even losses if entrepreneurs turn out to be poor performers in the early stage, but in which future prospects of returns in the later stage far outweigh initial investment costs. Borrowers in these circumstances can lend the amounts necessary for their operations and investments in business growth. Consequently, lenders and borrowers can share their firms' future surplus. In contrast, lenders in competitive credit markets cannot expect to recover initial subsidies via higher interest rate in the later stage, and therefore are forced to charge high interest rates in the early stage due to borrowers' opacity, which discourages their incentives and might cause their withdrawal from the lending relationship. Interbank competition enables borrowers to more easily switch to counterpart lenders, and thus, lenders must offer credit contracts on a period-by-period basis. Hence, interbank competition decreases lenders' profits from relationship lending.

Similar to Petersen and Rajan (1995), Hauswald and Marquez (2006) provide a model in which lenders enter into credit markets and invest their resources to collect borrower-specific information. This addresses greater interbank competition, which induces less investment information acquisition, and thus, lower interest rates. As competitors enter the market, greater interbank competition reduces the returns from information acquisition, and hence, each bank is forced to decrease its investment in screening technologies. The decline in informational content accumulated through credit screening softens the adverse selection problem against competitors, and encourages them to extend their captive markets, thus decreasing interest rates.

In a similar vein, Boot and Thakor's (2000) work is viewed as a prime motivating force in a series of studies on interbank competition and relationship lending. It provides a thorough revision of relationship lending literature and raises a further crucial research question regarding whether relationship lending is compatible with interbank competition. The authors provide a model in which lenders are engaged in both transaction-based and relationship lending to first investigate how much of the total loan is allocated to transaction-based and relationship lending. Second, their work examines how much effort is made in establishing and maintaining intimate relationships. This reveals competition's absolute effect on relationship lending, in that interbank competition provokes decreased lender profits from relationship lending. It also illustrates competition's relative (substitution) effect on relationship lending, in that the proportion of relationship loans to total lending increases. Further, interbank competition induces a decrease in both lending methods' interest rates, but negatively impacts transaction-based lending profits more than that of relationship lending. This is due to the development and collection of soft information and monitoring through such intimate relationships, which results in an "insulation effect" as lenders are protected from pure price competition with non-lenders. This insulation effect protects the lender's privileged access to borrower-specific information by creating barriers against potential competitors, thus minimizing lenders' deteriorating profits.

Consequently, interbank competition encourages the "substitution effect," or the shifting of lenders away from transaction-based lending toward relationship lending. Relationship lending becomes more important with greater interbank competition, but lenders cannot devote significant efforts to each counterpart, which causes each loan to have less added value and profitability. Therefore, based on the rational predictions by Boot and Thakor (2000), the authors provide the following hypotheses regarding interbank competition's influence on loan profitability and soft information investments:

Hypothesis 2.2 *Lenders in local markets with high interbank competition will face lower profitability.*

Hypothesis 2.3 *Local market competition primarily motivates lenders to acquire an investment advantage through exclusive relationship lending, which involves obtaining and using soft information.*

Hypothesis 2.4 *Although interbank competition negatively affects loan profitability, lenders in competitive local markets can acquire an informational advantage to limit their own losses through relationship lending.*

Literature commonly acknowledges interbank competition's negative impact on loan interest rates. For example, empirical results from De Nicolò et al. (2006) demonstrated a negative and statistically significant relationship between interbank competition (inverse Herfindahl-Hirschman index, or HHI, which is calculated in this work by squaring the market share of each bank competing in a market and then summing the resulting numbers)[5] and the rate of return on assets (ROA) in a sample of 2,500 U.S. banks that operated in rural non-Metropolitan Statistical Areas in 2003. De Nicolò and Loukoianova (2007) used 133 countries' individual bank data—excluding major developed countries—for the period of 1993 to 2004 to find no robust relationship exists between the ROA and concentration (HHI) when joint effects of bank ownership and market structure are not considered. In considering the influences of bank ownership and market structure, private domestic banks' ROA significantly improves in response to an increase in the HHI from both private domestic banks and foreign bank competitors. These results can be interpreted to denote that an increase in market segmentation allows banks to enhance their local market power, and the associated rents through this channel can boost their profitability.

Other research has empirically proven how interbank competition impacts investments in borrower-specific information. Degryse and Ongena (2007) used 9,858 Belgian borrowers' data from 1997 to analyze interbank competition's influence on relationship lending; their work indicated that fiercely competitive environments—or

[5]The HHI is widely used as a measure of concentration in the literature; Petersen and Rajan (1995), for example, employ the HHI as a measure of commercial bank deposit concentration for the county or Metropolitan Statistical Area where the firm is headquartered, while in Boot and Thakor (2000) the number of banks and hence by extension the HHI delineates the degree of competition in their model (Degryse and Ongena 2007).

the HHI, based on the number of branches in a borrower's district— encourage lenders to lean toward relationship lending. The degree of specialization in relationship lending is determined by its duration and scope, according to both Boot (2000) and Ongena and Smith (2000). The duration is measured by the length of the transaction period, and the scope of the engagement between a lender and borrower is captured by multiple product contracts as well as high turnover on the borrower's checking accounts.

However, soft information-based lending's effects on loan performance under interbank competition have yet to be empirically proven. This is primarily due to the difficulties in lender-side data availability, not only for investments in borrower-specific information, but also for profits generated from such investments.

2.3 The Informational Advantage of Relationship-Based Lending and Regional Banks' Credit Analysis Skills

An information advantage gained from collecting and using soft information could enable lenders to more accurately predict borrowers' risk of delinquency and default; hence, this could allow lenders to reduce loan-related losses from ex-post loan non-performance. Lenders could also observe borrowers' business operations to assess their effective use of loans through the monitoring process in relationship lending. By monitoring borrowers' activities to determine their compliance with contractual agreements—and enforcing the agreements in the case of noncompliance—lenders can reduce borrowers' incentives to commit moral hazards; they can discipline borrowers to deter their investments through opportunistic spending loans, and promote prudent investment behaviors. Thus, lenders can prevent borrowers from taking risk at the former's expense and decrease the probability of delays or an inability to repay the lender's principal and interest. This leads to the following hypothesis:

Hypothesis 2.5 *Lenders who highly value the collecting and using of soft information obtain lower bad loan ratios on average.*

Some research has shown support for this hypothesis. De Young et al. (2008), for example, randomly sampled 29,577 small business loans from 5,535 lenders from 1984 to 2001 to find that geographic proximity, which allows lenders to observe and accumulate soft information, contributes to a decrease in the probability of loan default. On the other hand, Jiménez and Saurina (2004) offered opposing empirical evidence in their research on using soft information in loans greater than €24,000 provided to companies in Spain from 1987 to 2000. The authors discovered that close relationships increase the probability of default, assuming that a lender-borrower relationship becomes strong when a borrower's loans are not spread across several or many financial institutions. They interpreted this result to mean that lenders are prepared to finance riskier borrowers with higher default rates ex-post if they can subsequently offset the loan losses resulting from higher default rates by applying higher interest rates to the surviving borrowers.[6] Their work also indicated that lenders are willing to finance higher-risk loans if they have close relationships with their borrowers, as these lenders might provide a large percentage of the borrower's finances, or might even be the only bank to finance them. This suggests that a greater degree of commitment exists if lenders can subsequently recoup greater expected losses by charging higher interest rates to their other surviving exclusive (or nearly exclusive) borrowers.

2.4 Interbank Competition's Effect on Loan Risk

As Boyd and De Nicoló (2005) first noted, one dominant notion in banking is that a lender in a concentrated market can earn monopolistic rents and thus become relatively conservative, maintaining its banking charter. These monopolistic rents can make banking franchises more valuable, and their insolvency will become costlier. The underlying source of a franchise's value is assumed to be its market power, and thus, reduced competition has been considered to promote banking stability (Jiménez et al. 2013). If a lender confronts increasing competition, in other words, its market power erodes and its profit margin decreases. This results in a reduced franchise value that exacerbates potential moral hazards, and hence, the lender will intentionally assume more credit risk. This is the traditional "competition-fragility" perspective (Berger et al. 2009).

Nevertheless, and in contrast to this notion, Boyd and De Nicoló (2005) reveal a lender's fundamental risk-incentive mechanism, which causes the lender to assume more risk as its market becomes more concentrated, resulting in higher risk of default. As a lender's power increases in the loan market, it can use this monopoly power to increase loan rates *ceteris paribus*, even after considering the fact that borrowers will invest in riskier projects in conjunction with higher financing costs. A higher interest rate may also induce the borrower's moral hazard to result in a high risk of default, which could lead to a high loan delinquency rate. Monopoly power may lead to banking instability, as higher interest rates also attract a riskier set of borrowers, resulting in adverse selection (Berger et al. 2009). Conversely, a lender's risk of failure strictly decreases in the number of competing firms (De Nicoló et al. 2006). An appropriately competitive loan rate reinforces the borrower's disciplined investments, an alternative that has been called the "competition-stability" perspective (Berger et al. 2009). These lead to the following hypothesis:

---

[6]Sharpe (1990) illustrated why a lender might commit to a distressed borrower by introducing the concept of "reputation," which demonstrates that a lender might lend to a distressed borrower if a surplus can be shared in the long-term. A lender can earn economic rents using its ex-post monopoly power over a captive borrower during the intertemporal period. Further, a lender can build and maintain a good reputation by keeping a non-binding commitment with an incumbent lender through intimate interactions, so that future potential borrowers can learn of the lender's propensity to keep promises.

Hypothesis 2.6 *Lenders in local markets with higher interbank competition have proportionally higher bad loan ratios, and* vice versa.

Rhoades (1977) reviewed early literature on U.S. markets with samples from the 1960s to 1970s which provided empirical evidence showing a negative relationship between market concentration and non-performing loan ratios—a proxy indicator for the risk of default. This is consistent with the traditional "competition-fragility" perspective. Further, De Young et al. (2008) sampled small business loans to find that interbank competition causes high probabilities of loan default. These results suggest that lenders under interbank competition are less likely to cultivate relationships with their small business borrowers, such as through perfunctory screening and monitoring procedures, which can exacerbate loans' rates of default.

Alternatively, De Nicoló et al. (2006) provided empirical results regarding the negative, statistically significant relationship between the probability of bank failure[7] and interbank competition (inverse HHI) in a 2003 sample of 2,500 U.S. banks; this sampling revealed a positive relationship between interbank competition and bank stability. De Nicolò and Loukoianova's (2007) work also found a negative, significant relationship between the probability of bank failure (see footnote 7) and interbank competition (inverse HHI). This relationship also holds when it substitutes a risk measure with the ratio of nonperforming to gross loans. These two articles support the alternative "competition-stability" perspective.

Berger et al. (2009) emphasize that these two strands of literature need not necessarily yield opposite predictions regarding market competition's influence on bank stability. Even if a lender obtains market power and accepts riskier loan portfolios, it can offset the higher loan risk exposure through more equity capital, reduced interest rate risk, and the sales of loans or credit derivatives, among other risk-mitigating techniques. Therefore, studies' adequate choice of dependent variables becomes increasingly important to reflect either or both loan or bank risks in analyzing interbank competition's effect on bank risk, thereby distinguishing whether one or both views can be applied. Berger et al. (2009) demonstrated this argument by regressing measures of loan risk and bank risk on several measures of market power, as well as indicators of the business environment, using data from 1999 to 2005 in over 30 developed countries. This principle firstly reveals that—consistent with the alternative "competition-stability" perspective—the degree of market power positively affects the ratio of nonperforming loans to total loans (NPLs), which is a proxy of loan risk. This relationship is analyzed using three measures of market concentration in its regressions: the Lerner index, the HHI deposit, and the HHI loan indices. The NPL regression indicates that the coefficient of the HHI deposit index is significantly positive, and that of the square term for the HHI deposit index is significantly nega-

[7]The Z-score is used to empirically measure risk, and specifically, the probability of bank failure. The Z-score measure for bank risk equals the rate of return on assets plus the ratio of equity to assets, divided by the standard deviation of the rate of return on assets. This risk measure is monotonously associated with the measure of lenders' probability of failure, and thus, empirical banking and finance literature has widely used this measure. It combines profitability, leverage, and return volatility in a single measure, and a decreased Z-score denotes higher risk.

tive, with a parabolic curve that opens downward. This also demonstrates that 99% of the data lie below the highest point of the parabola. The result using the HHI loan index as the independent variable also indicates a significant positive association between the NPLs and the HHI loan index. These results indicate that high market competition is associated with low loan risk, supporting the "competition-stability" perspective.

Berger et al.'s (2009) principle secondly reveals that—consistent with the traditional "competition-fragility" perspective—the degree of market power has a negative effect on the Z-score (see footnote 7), which is used as an inverse proxy for overall bank risk; a higher value indicates greater bank stability. The regressions for the Z-score show that the coefficients for all three measures of market concentration—the Lerner index, the HHI deposit, and the HHI loan indices—are significantly positive, and all from the quadratic term are significantly negative. An analysis demonstrates that 99% of the data lie below the highest point of the parabola, which opens downward. These results suggest that high market competition is associated with an overall high bank instability. The results support the "competition-fragility" perspective, in that interbank competition could erode the franchise value derived from its market power, and encourage banks to increase their overall risk exposure.

Berger et al.'s (2009) results of market concentration on loan risk exposure and overall bank risk show that interbank competition reduces loan portfolio risk, but accelerates overall bank risk. Banks might be forced to lower their loan rates due to interbank competition and subsequently decrease their loan portfolio risk, while simultaneously expanding their business into areas other than loans to compensate for the lost opportunities for profit in their loans.

2.5 Interbank Competitions and the Effect of Relationship Lending on Bad Loan Ratios

Interbank competition deprives incumbent lenders of incentives to acquire borrower-specific information due to the decline of expected interest rates, resulting in lower-quality loan screening and monitoring capabilities. Insufficient credit assessments not only cause fewer efficient lending decisions, resulting in riskier loan-portfolio choices, but also allow borrowers to engage in moral-hazard behavior, thereby increasing default rates. Hauswald and Marquez's (2006) model involved lenders entering credit markets to invest their resources and collect borrower-specific information; the authors found that price competition-driven, lower-than-expected interest rates reduce informational investments, which consequently lead to less-efficient credit allocation and deteriorated aggregate loan quality.

Certainly, interbank competition discourages incumbent lenders' incentives to generate information, and decreases the threat of adverse selection for potential entrants, but information barriers could still deter potential rivals from entering local credit markets. Even if the threat of adverse selection for rivals decreases, it could still effectively function, to a certain degree. Under interbank competition, less-efficient lending decisions and the deterioration of credit loan portfolios might be inevitable, but information barriers could help insulate incumbent lenders to some degree from the threat of new entrants. Thus,

Hypothesis 2.7 *Lenders within competitive local markets that acquire an information advantage become insulated from interbank competition despite a lower average loan quality, and* vice versa.

Bofondi and Gobbi's (2006) work used a database with 7,275 observations of 729 Italian banks from 1986 to 1996. The authors analyzed the differences in loan default rates between incumbent and entrant lenders to find that the default rates for lenders entering local markets was significantly higher than those for incumbent lenders. Moreover, it has been argued that information entry barriers function efficiently to bar entrant lenders from the local credit market; the number of entrants into the local credit market remains low, as such an entry can be accompanied by substantial costs. The article also demonstrates that the default rates are lower for lenders that enter by opening a branch than those that enter without. This suggests that having a branch on-site can help decrease any informational disadvantage, as a geographic lender–borrower proximity signifies the degree of specialization in relationship lending. Incumbent lenders have proprietary information about borrowers' risk characteristics, and thus, "skim the cream" from local markets by forcing entrants to lend to riskier borrowers.

2.6 Conclusions

This chapter provides a recent survey of literature regarding relationship lending's influence on lender performance, specifically in competitive local credit markets, and subsequently yields the following hypotheses on this theme. At its most fundamental, the lender's role is to provide funds to informationally opaque SMEs that face severe financial constraints due to informational asymmetries. Lenders initiate the necessary production of information through lender–borrower relationships. Information such as data stored internally within the firm or those transferred among the local networks gained over time. Banks' important role in this case is expected to resolve problems in providing external sources to informationally opaque SMEs (Berger et al. 2001), while information asymmetries simultaneously create substantial profitable opportunities for local lenders. Incumbent lenders can create information barriers for non-lenders, and non-lenders face an adverse selection problem that can deter them from entering the lending relationship; thus, borrowers are forced to lock themselves into an entrenched lender–borrower nexus. Therefore, the authors first hypothesized that incumbent lenders can create ex-post monopoly power and charge high interest rates to informationally captured borrowers.

Additionally, the information advantage derived from collecting and using soft information could ensure lenders' more accurate predictions of borrowers' risk of delinquency and default; this will allow lenders to reduce loan-related losses from ex-post loan non-performance. Consequently, the authors then hypothesized that lenders with an informational advantage gained through the lender–borrower relationship obtain lower bad loan ratios.

A central question in this book involves whether interbank competition influences lenders' loan performance. As competitors enter the market, greater interbank competition reduces the returns from acquiring information, and hence, this compels each bank to decrease its investments in screening technologies. As a result, interbank competition decreases lenders' profits from relationship lending, which further results in a high loan delinquency rate. Therefore, the authors second hypothesized that lenders in local markets with higher interbank competition face lower profitability and proportionally higher bad loan ratios. However, the development and collection of soft information and monitoring through such intimate relationships might protect incumbent lenders' privileged access to borrower-specific information through barriers against potential competitors, thus minimizing lenders' profit deterioration. Thus, the authors' third hypothesis posits that interbank competition motivates lenders to acquire an investment advantage through exclusive relationship lending; this enables them to limit their own losses. Further, it can be hypothesized that creating information barriers against non-lenders might help incumbent lenders alleviate an escalating loan delinquency rate.

Chapter 4 tests these basic hypotheses as proposed by the authors. Prior to their multivariate analyses, the authors provide a general overview of Japanese banking industry, including its restructuring and current status, both of which involved significant market entries and exits.

References

Berger, A. N., & Hannan, T. H. (1989). The price-concentration relationship in banking. *The Review of Economics and Statistics, 71*(2), 291–299.

Berger, A. N., Klapper, L. F., & Turk-Ariss, R. (2009). Bank competition and financial stability. *Journal of Financial Services Research, 35*(2), 99–118.

Berger, A. N., Klapper, L. F., & Udell, G. F. (2001). The ability of banks to lend to informationally opaque small businesses. *Journal of Banking & Finance, 25*(12), 2127–2167.

Bofondi, M., & Gobbi, G. (2006). Informational barriers to entry into credit markets. *Review of Finance, 10*(1), 39–67.

Boot, A. W. (2000). Relationship banking: What do we know? *Journal of Financial Intermediation, 9*(1), 7–25.

Boot, A. W., & Thakor, A. V. (2000). Can relationship banking survive competition? *The Journal of Finance, 55*(2), 679–713.

Boyd, J. H., & De Nicolo, G. (2005). The theory of bank risk taking and competition revisited. *The Journal of finance, 60*(3), 1329–1343.

Carter, D. A., & McNulty, J. E. (2005). Deregulation, technological change, and the business-lending performance of large and small banks. *Journal of Banking & Finance, 29*(5), 1113–1130.

Carter, D. A., McNulty, J. E., & Verbrugge, J. A. (2004). Do small banks have an advantage in lending? An examination of risk-adjusted yields on business loans at large and small banks. *Journal of Financial Services Research, 25*(2–3), 233–252.

De Nicolò, G., & Loukoianova, E. (2007). *Bank ownership, market structure and risk*. IMF Working Papers No. 07/215. International Monetary Fund.
De Nicoló, M. G., Jalal, A. M., & Boyd, J. H. (2006). *Bank risk-taking and competition revisited: New theory and new evidence*. IMF Working Papers No. 06/297. International Monetary Fund.
Degryse, H., & Ongena, S. (2007). The impact of competition on bank orientation. *Journal of Financial Intermediation, 16*(3), 399–424.
DeYoung, R., Glennon, D., & Nigro, P. (2008). Borrower–lender distance, credit scoring, and loan performance: Evidence from informational-opaque small business borrowers. *Journal of Financial Intermediation, 17*(1), 113–143.
Diamond, D. W. (1991). Monitoring and reputation: The choice between bank loans and directly placed debt. *Journal of Political Economy, 99*(4), 689–721.
Ergungor, O. E. (2005). The profitability of bank–borrower relationships. *Journal of Financial Intermediation, 14*(4), 485–512.
Greenbaum, S. I., Kanatas, G., & Venezia, I. (1989). Equilibrium loan pricing under the bank-client relationship. *Journal of Banking & Finance, 13*(2), 221–235.
Hauswald, R., & Marquez, R. (2006). Competition and strategic information acquisition in credit markets. *The Review of Financial Studies, 19*(3), 967–1000.
Jiménez, G., Lopez, J. A., & Saurina, J. (2013). How does competition affect bank risk-taking? *Journal of Financial Stability, 9*(2), 185–195.
Jiménez, G., & Saurina, J. (2004). Collateral, type of lender and relationship banking as determinants of credit risk. *Journal of Banking & Finance, 28*(9), 2191–2212.
Ongena, S., & Smith, D. C. (2000). What determines the number of bank relationships? Cross-country evidence. *Journal of Financial Intermediation, 9*(1), 26–56.
Petersen, M. A., & Rajan, R. G. (1995). The effect of credit market competition on lending relationships. *The Quarterly Journal of Economics, 110*(2), 407–443.
Rhoades, S. A. (1977). Structure-performance studies in banking: A summary and evaluation. *Staff Studies, 92*. Board of Governors of the Federal Reserve System.
Schenone, C. (2010). Lending relationships and information rents: Do banks exploit their information advantages? *The Review of Financial Studies, 23*(3), 1149–1199.
Schwarze, F. (2007). Relationship banking and profitability - An empirical survey of German banks. Retrieved from http://dx.doi.org/10.2139/ssrn.967235.
Sharpe, S. A. (1990). Asymmetric information, bank lending, and implicit contracts: A stylized model of customer relationships. *The Journal of Finance, 45*(4), 1069–1087.
Stiglitz, J. E., & Weiss, A. (1981). Credit rationing in markets with imperfect information. *The American Economic Review, 71*(3), 393–410.
Stiglitz, J. E., & Weiss, A. (1983). Incentive effects of terminations: Applications to the credit and labor markets. *The American Economic Review, 73*(5), 912–927.
Storey, D. J. (2016). *Understanding the small business sector*. London and New York: Routledge.
Uehara, K. (2007). The challenges of financing in SMEs: Efforts to utilize the asset based lending (Chusho kigyo ni okeru shikin chotatsu no kadai: Urikake saiken tanpo oyobi dosan tanpo no katsuyo ni mukete, in Japanese). *The Prism of Economy (Keizai no purizumu in Japanese), 38*, 1–10.
Vos, E., Yeh, A. J.-Y., Carter, S., & Tagg, S. (2007). The happy story of small business financing. *Journal of Banking & Finance, 31*(9), 2648–2672.

Chapter 3
Survey Data from Japanese Regional Banks and Using Soft Information in Lending Decisions

Abstract This book investigates the role of relationship lending in Japanese local competitive markets. The authors used data from a 2008 survey by the Organization for Small and Medium Enterprises and Regional Innovation, Japan (SME Support, Japan) to extract soft information factors from questionnaire answers relative to the use of soft information in making lending decisions. Ultimately, the authors analyzed the influence of using soft information on lender performance. Therefore, this chapter first provides an overview of Japanese banking institutions as well as the characteristics of the small and medium-sized/regional financial institutions that comprise the analysis sample: regional banks, second-tier regional banks, and shinkin banks. Second, this chapter describes the survey questionnaire's objectives and methods, and presents regional institutions' current status regarding their use of soft information. Third, the chapter explains the factor analysis and the procedures to determine the number of underlying factors and retain the items that correlate to them. This chapter then incorporates the univariate analysis to further report the preliminary results of soft information's influence on lender performance.

Keywords Regional banks · Second-tier regional banks · Shinkin banks · Factor analysis · Latent factor · Soft information · Organizational systems · Networks or alliances/partnerships · Business and management leadership

3.1 Characteristics of Japanese Banks

Japan's depository financial institutions are conventionally classified into eight categories: mega banks, long-term credit banks, trust banks, regional banks, second-tier regional banks, shinkin banks (formerly called "credit associations"), credit cooperatives, and agricultural and forestry cooperatives.

In the context of this article, it is important to note that the institutions in the latter five categories operate their businesses in certain restricted local areas, while the former three have nationwide branch office networks. Regional banks, second-tier regional banks, shinkin banks, credit cooperatives, and agricultural and forestry cooperatives typically operate within a single prefecture or administrative region;

T. Yosano and T. Nakaoka, *Utilization of Soft Information on Bank Performance*, Development Bank of Japan Research Series,
https://doi.org/10.1007/978-981-13-8472-1_3

on average, 81.1% of regional and second-tier regional bank branches are located within the same prefecture as their head office, while 95.8% of shinkin bank branches operate in their home prefecture. Regional bank deposit and loan markets remain geographically segmented in Japan (Kano and Tsutsui 2003) even after the Japanese financial system's drastic deregulation and liberalization from the 1980s to the early 2000s, and these types of banks act as critical capital providers to local businesses. Moreover, banks accumulate valuable information on their clientele through mutual interactions with local businesses, and establish close-knit relationships with them as well as the local community.

This institutional background indicates that regional banks were designed to effectively function as essential capital providers for local businesses, and this has been regulated under Japan's Banking Act. Such institutions operate in each of the country's 47 prefectures and are normally headquartered in the prefectural capital. Further, they conduct the majority of their business within a given prefecture, and act as an important source of credit to SMEs (Liu and Wilson 2013). Savings banks were transformed into second-tier regional banks in 1989, and were brought under the umbrella of the Banking Act that applied to regional banks. These former savings banks specialize in small business loans, but no longer need to follow the currently outdated rules. However, most of their clientele in practice are local, small firms (Schaede 2005).

Shinkin banks are depository institutions and form cooperative regional financial networks based on non-profit and mutual aid membership schemes in compliance with the Shinkin Bank Act. Any SME—with less than or an equivalent of 300 employees, or 900 million yen in capital—with an office in the region is eligible for membership. Shinkin banks limit their lending in principle to their members, but in practice their functions are nearly the same as those of commercial banks: they accept deposits from members and non-members, and make loans to members and graduated members—those who have outgrown membership qualifications. Credit cooperatives are also depository institutions, organized under the 1949 Law for Small Business Cooperatives, and are principally based on the mutual support of SME owners and employees. Any SME—with 100 or fewer employees or 100 million yen in capital for wholesalers, 50 employees or 50 million yen for retailers, 100 employees or 50 million yen for services, and 300 employees or 300 million yen for other industries—with an office in the region is eligible for membership. These entities accept deposits from members and lend to members and certain nonmembers, although loans to nonmembers are limited to 20% of their total loans. Credit cooperatives are distinctly characterized by their main customers, which are primarily micro-businesses, SMEs, and workers in these companies; thus, their customer size is much smaller than that of shinkin banks.

The unprecedented escalation of non-performing loans in the Japanese banking sector during the 1990s triggered the large-scale reorganization of banks through mergers and closures. Figure 3.1 illustrates the evolution of Japan's number of depository institutions with the number of mega banks dramatically decreasing, from 13 in 1989 to 6 in 2008. Shinkin banks also radically decreased through mergers and closures, from 454 in 1989 to 279 in 2008. In addition to the slowdown that followed

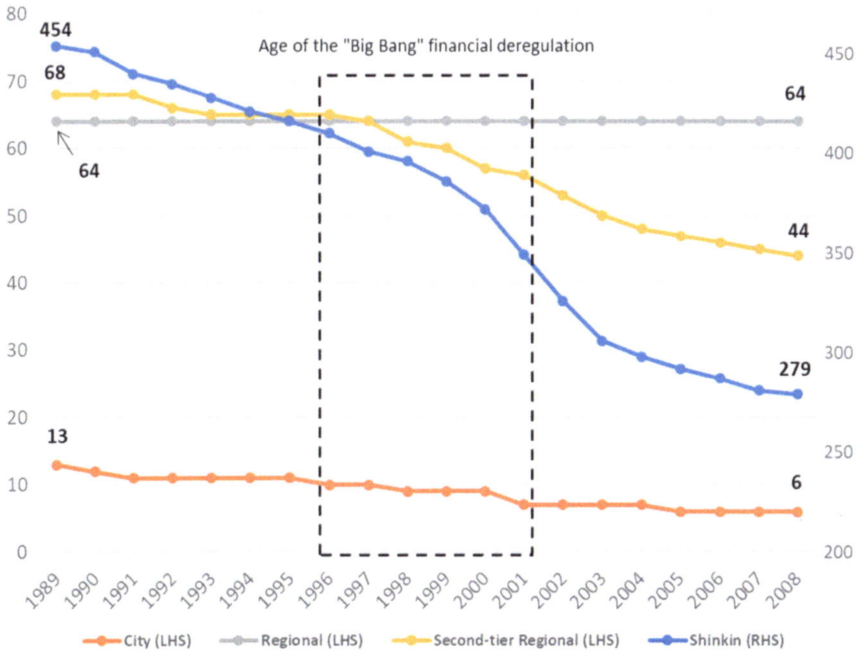

Fig. 3.1 The evolution of Japan's number of depository institutions. *Source* Deposit Insurance Corporation of Japan, https://www.dic.go.jp/, accessed November 2018

the country's economic boom in the 1980s, the financial liberalization that began in 1984 (Osugi 1990) has accelerated interbank competition. Financial deregulation has occurred in such areas as vested interest rates, financial market segmentation, and barriers to foreign banks' market entry. Almost all bank deposit rates had been liberalized by 1993 (Horiuchi 1996), while entry controls among the banking, securities, and insurance industries had been removed by 2001 through the "Big Bang" deregulatory reform program initiated in 1996.[1] The liberalization of the foreign exchange business—such as liberalized foreign transactions beginning in 1990 (Fukao 1990) and liberalized cross-border capital transactions in 1998 (Bank of Japan 1998), as well as the liberalization of the interest rate ceiling and introduction of cross-entries among financial sectors, brought newcomers to the Japanese financial market.

[1]The post-war period for Japan's financial system existed from the 1950s to the late 1970s. One characteristic of Japan's post-war financial system was its rigid segmentation by regulation. The businesses in which each financial institution could engage was limited by laws, orders, and administrative guidance. The separation between banking and trust businesses, and between long-term and short-term banking, was a salient feature of the Japanese financial system (Osugi 1990; Mabuchi 1993). This helped mobilize financial resources into prioritized industries in Japan's high-growth era.

Compared to the sharp decrease in the number of mega and shinkin banks, the number of regional banks slightly decreased, from 68 in 1989 to 64 in 2008. Regional banks operate in accordance with the policy of one regional bank per prefecture, or two at the most, advocated by the Financial Service Agency in Japan (FSA). Therefore, regional banks have been able to play a core role of finance in their localities through the longtime lender–borrower relationship, as well as a lengthy period of support and promotion of local industries. Building a local presence over a long period insulated them from interbank competition, which intensified until the late 1980s. Second-tier regional banks experienced a decrease in number of over 30%, from 68 in 1989 to 45 in 2008, which demonstrated a greater decline than regional banks. As second-tier regional banks had insufficient capital, with less capital surplus and less retained earnings than regional banks, they were more vulnerable to swollen non-performing loans due to the economic recession (Yoshimoto 2013).

3.2 Survey Description and a Data Sample

This book uses data from a 2008 survey by the "Working Group on Intellectual Asset-Based Finance for Small and Medium-Sized Enterprises" under the "Study Group on Intellectual Asset-Based Management for Small and Medium-Sized Enterprises" established in 2007 at SME Support, Japan. This survey aimed to investigate how and to what extent Japan's banking sector used non-financial information in lending decisions as well as in its business support programs. The scrutiny of borrowers through the application process involves four main phases: the borrower-bank search, credit analysis, credit risk assessment and valuation for loans, and the establishment of monitoring policies. This survey covers the latter three phases, with the final goal of providing a foundation for strengthening SME lending based on non-financial information, paralleling the action program introduced in 2003. This FSA action program required small and medium-sized/regional financial institutions to shift from transaction-based lending to relationship lending. This program encouraged lenders to primarily judge SMEs' creditworthiness based on a business assessment—an observation of their businesses' strengths and weaknesses—without relying on collateral assets from the SME loans market. The program was expected to tighten the lender–borrower relationship and ensure the soundness of both lenders and borrowers. This book specifically uses the survey questionnaire data to categorize questionnaire items into three soft information factors: organizational systems, networks or alliances/partnerships, and business and management leadership by a factor analysis.

Before the working group sent questionnaires to financial institutions, it conducted preliminary interview surveys on six regional financial institutions selected in late 2007, and the author, who was a member of the working group, accompanied the interview team. The interview team collected comprehensive non-financial information items generally used in the credit risk assessment and business support program. The working group listed up to 54 non-financial information items in accordance with the preliminary interviews, and inserted those items into the questionnaire as questions scored using five-point Likert scales. Questionnaires were mailed to all 575 financial institutions as of early 2008 (6 mega banks, 64 regional banks, 45 second-tier regional banks, 282 shinkin banks, 145 credit cooperatives, and 33 others), and 428 responded (6 mega banks, 76 regional and second-tier regional banks, 244 shinkin banks, 98 credit cooperatives, and 4 others), with a response rate of 76.3%. A follow-up phone call was conducted to all financial institutions that did not respond by the deadline to improve the response rate. The questions regarded the degree to which financial institutions use both in their lending decisions and in business support among 54 non-financial items categorized into the following 7 groups: (1) human capital (top management); (2) external business environments; (3) business content; (4) customers and suppliers; (5) human capital (employees); (6) foundations of management, such as its philosophy, business model, and employee evaluation system; and (7) risk management and the corporate governance structure.

As this book focuses on the use of soft information in the lending decision, the authors selected 38 soft information items from 54 non-financial items in the 2008 questionnaire survey conducted by SME Support, Japan (see Appendix 3.1). Financial information involves all financial figures from financial statements, including footnotes, supplemental information, and indices based on financial figures, while information other than financial information is considered non-financial information. Soft information has much in common with non-financial information, but the former is defined by unquantifiable, unverifiable, and sometimes subjective information (see Sect. 1.3). Lenders gather and process qualitative information where necessary—such as managerial competencies, key customers' status, and employees' expertise—to assess borrowers' creditworthiness. This information is gathered in the course of personal interactions between lenders and borrowers, and such information is called "soft" information when it is proprietary and subjective, and difficult to quantify. Therefore, the authors first focused on 38 types of soft information among 54 non-financial items, and second conducted a factor analysis.

This book adopts a factor analysis to discover the latent factors that create commonalities, especially as several pieces of information convey a sense of cleavage or division. The factor analysis extracts three principal factors: (1) the organizational system, (2) networks or alliances/partnerships, and (3) business and management leadership. Table 3.1 expresses each soft information item's relationship to these three underlying factors. The personnel evaluation system has the strongest association with its underlying latent factor—the organizational system—with a factor loading of 0.868.[2] Items with factor loadings of less than 0.4 for all three factors were excluded from the sample, reducing the number of items in the study to 22 items (see Table 3.1).

[2]Each item's relationship to the underlying factor is expressed by its factor loading.

Table 3.1 Factor analysis of soft information

	1	2	3	Mean value: five-point likert scale	Standard deviation	Categories: SME Support, Japan
Organizational systems						
Personnel evaluation system	**0.868**	0.139	−0.011	2.794	0.548	Organizational foundation
Company-specific improvement reporting system/the number of improvements	**0.819**	0.146	0.023	2.858	0.545	Organizational foundation
Incentive system	**0.718**	0.098	−0.018	2.774	0.581	Employees
Enhancement level of corporate education	**0.674**	0.113	0.226	3.003	0.531	Organizational foundation
IT system equipment	**0.640**	0.032	0.294	3.048	0.552	Organizational foundation
Efficient labor–management relations	**0.611**	0.237	0.176	3.100	0.585	Organizational foundation
Employee knowledge	**0.535**	0.147	0.223	3.232	0.621	Employees
Networks or alliances/partnerships						
Supplier relationships	0.239	**0.807**	0.161	3.336	0.537	Customers/suppliers
Customer relationships	0.223	**0.727**	0.223	3.439	0.592	Customers/suppliers
Supplier status	0.042	**0.706**	0.302	3.461	0.583	Customers/suppliers
Customer status	−0.012	**0.623**	0.378	3.671	0.598	Customers/suppliers
Managers' seniority	0.181	**0.506**	0.234	3.390	0.574	Manager
Management has industrial experience	0.128	**0.497**	0.234	3.342	0.591	Manager
Manager networks	0.251	**0.456**	0.274	3.277	0.546	Manager

(continued)

Table 3.1 (continued)

	1	2	3	Mean value: five-point likert scale	Standard deviation	Categories: SME Support, Japan
Business and management leadership						
Management capability	0.070	0.107	**0.590**	3.923	0.575	Manager
Business plan	0.035	0.200	**0.569**	3.977	0.588	Organizational foundation
Managers' personality traits	0.078	0.265	**0.547**	3.748	0.650	Manager
Advantage in the core business	0.083	0.375	**0.509**	3.890	0.581	Business contents
Management leadership	0.220	0.272	**0.501**	3.494	0.579	Manager
Management philosophy	0.324	0.173	**0.496**	3.490	0.573	Organizational foundation
Technological superiority	0.118	0.211	**0.461**	3.884	0.557	Business contents
Managerial succession	0.104	0.231	**0.445**	3.977	0.548	Manager
Eigenvalue	6.973	2.709	1.227			
Percent of variance (%)	43.350	16.840	7.630			
No. of observations	310					

Notes The authors compute the factor loading by determining the relationship of each questionnaire item from the SME Support, Japan survey to its corresponding communality through a varimax rotation; three underlying factors are extracted from the sample of 310 regional and shinkin banks in Japan: (1) organizational systems, (2) business and management leadership, and (3) networks or alliances/partnerships. The authors then test whether each item within a single factor highly correlates by performing a maximum likelihood confirmatory factor analysis. This reveals that the underlying three factors explain 67.82% of the total variance with eigenvalues of 6.973, 2.709, and 1.227, respectively, and have an average commonality of 0.460. These figures indicate that each item within a single factor could be singularly influential. The authors then further test the extent to which the three factors are distinct and uncorrelated by examining the pattern matrix; they find no cross-loadings exist, as no item cross-loads on another factor at a level greater than 0.40. This demonstrates that the three factors could have distinct constructs.

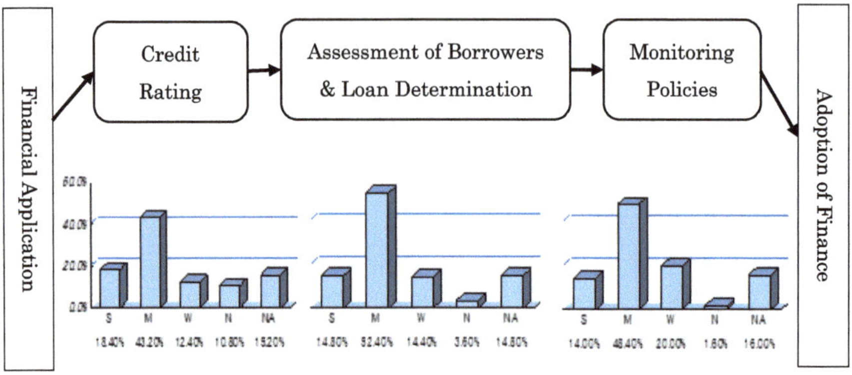

Fig. 3.2 Banks' usage levels of soft information in three loan application phases *Note* S = "strong use," M = "medium use," W = "weak use," N = "no use," and NA = "no reply."

Japan's depository financial institutions are classified into eight categories, and all these financial institutions were surveyed. However, mega banks, long-term credit banks, and trust banks operate nationwide, and prefectural-level data on their local operations are not available, while this book specifically focuses on interbank competition in local credit markets. Therefore, it excludes these three types of financial institutions from the sample. It also eliminates credit cooperatives from the sample due to their smaller customer size, and further excludes agricultural and forestry cooperatives due to their limited partnership clientele. Thus, the authors eventually construct a sample with 76 regional and second-tier regional banks and 244 shinkin banks, or a total of 310 banks.

3.3 Using Soft Information in Lending Decision Processes

The survey investigated the degree of soft information usage in three loan application processes: credit analyses, credit risk assessments and valuations for loans, and the establishment of monitoring policies. Figure 3.2 illustrates banks' usage levels of soft information in three loan application phases. Bank representatives answered questions regarding each item's usage level by marking check boxes for five-point Likert scale questions (S = "strong use," M = "medium use," W = "weak use," N = "no use," and NA = "no reply"). The credit analysis phase has the highest "strong use" of soft information at 18.40%, exceeding the credit risk assessment phase (14.80%) and policy-monitoring phase (14.00%) by 3.6% and 4.4%, respectively. On the other hand, the credit risk-assessment phase has the highest percentage of "medium use" at 52.40%, exceeding the credit analysis phase (43.20%) and policy-monitoring phase (48.40%) by 9.2% and 4.0%, respectively.

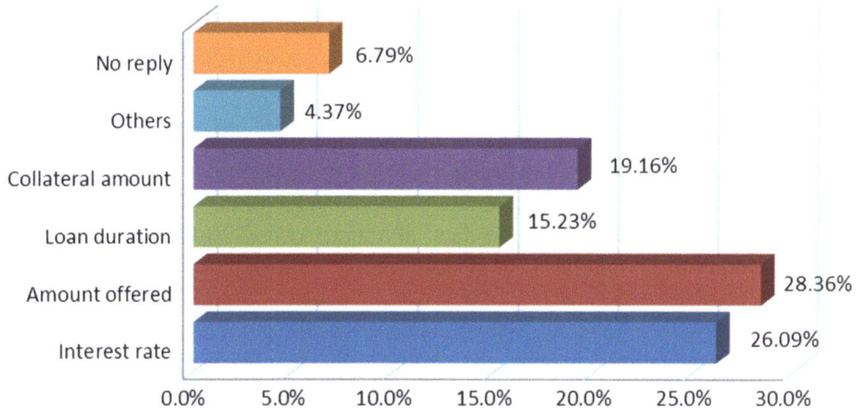

Fig. 3.3 Soft information's influence on credit conditions

Over 60% of regional and shinkin banks utilize soft information at a "strong use" or "medium use" level in all three phases. The highest phase of soft information use is the credit risk assessment phase, as 67.2% of banks use it with high or medium degrees of probability. These figures suggest that a majority of banks react positively in their lending decisions. However, the highest "strong use" level in the credit analysis phase (18.4%) further suggests that banks struggle to incorporate proprietary, subjective information in their credit analyses.

The survey also investigated whether soft information influences credit conditions, such as loan interest rates, the principal amount of the loan, duration of the loan period, and collateral value. Figure 3.3 displays the percentage of "yes" responses to "yes or no" questions regarding soft information's use in each credit condition. This figure reveals that regional and shinkin banks most conspicuously use soft information in their principal loan amounts, at 28.36%. They use soft information in determining their interest rates, with the second-highest percentage of 26.09%, and use it in their collateral values, with the third-highest percentage of 19.16%. Finally, they use soft information in determining credit periods, at 15.23%. These findings indicate that soft information substantially influences credit conditions, which addresses its important practical significance. Moreover, these figures parallel findings from pioneer research on soft information, such as works by Petersen and Rajan (1994) and Berger and Udell (1995), which analyze the benefits of relationship lending in loan conditions; they address relationship lending's potential contribution in lowering interest rates, amplifying credit availability, and decreasing collateral securities.

Regarding this book's main focus on 22 soft information items, the survey concludes by asking banks to indicate their usage levels for each item in the lending decision by marking checkboxes on five-point Likert scale questions, which range from one ("no use") to five ("considerable use"). Table 3.1 displays each soft information item, its Likert scale mean value and standard deviation, and label from the original survey's seven categories.

3.4 A Factor Analysis for Soft Information and Our Sample's Descriptive Data

This book conducted a factor analysis to determine the categorized information lenders emphasize in their lending decisions. Many previous researchers (Scott 2004; Ogura and Uchida 2014; Uchida et al. 2008) conducted a principal component analysis to extract components from the data, although no prior study to the authors' knowledge other than Uchida's (2011) has executed a factor analysis in the banking industry.[3]

Both statistical techniques are essentially based on the same statistical procedures: extraction, interpretation, rotation, and choosing the number of factors or components. Despite these similarities, a fundamental difference exists between the two analyses, as the factor analysis model measures a latent variable, while the principal component analysis model measures a principal component variable. This analysis can aggregate many observable variables into an intrinsic dimension within a multi-dimensional space that represents an underlying concept, making it easier to understand the data. In contrast, the principal component analysis is a linear combination of variables; it creates one or more index variables from a large set of measured variables. Its aggregation serves to efficiently extract information. In summary, the principal component analysis aims to reduce our correlated observed variables to a smaller set of important independent composite variables, while the factor analysis assumes a single latent variable associated with multiple observed variables with similar response patterns.

This book conducted a factor analysis, as the authors' motivation involves using the survey data to discover unobserved latent factors in financial organizations. The extraction stage involves procedures to determine the number of underlying factors and retain the items that correlate to them. This study ultimately excluded 12 items uncorrelated to the three underlying factors from its analyses: organizational systems, business and management leadership, and networks or alliances/partnerships (see Sect. 5.4 for more detail definitions based on a review of management literature). In deciding the number of factors, eigenvalues were adopted as criteria, as these reveal the variance explained by that particular factor from the total variance, and the threshold for this criteria is that the eigenvalue must be greater than one. Therefore, the authors have no ex ante information on the latent factors themselves or their quantity. This exploratory factor analysis is a subset of the multivariate analysis.

[3]Uchida (2011) applied a factor analysis to data on loan screening for SMEs in Japan, and discovered that banks emphasize three factors when deciding whether to grant loans: the relationship, financial statement, and collateral/guarantee factors. This book applies the same statistical procedure to the questionnaire data.

The degree of soft information used depends on the latent factors that represent how the bank as an entire organization emphasizes soft information. Soft information is unquantifiable, unverifiable, and sometimes subjective, and therefore, essentially consists of abstract concepts. A factor analysis enables us to measure these latent variables that correspond to abstract concepts; thus, the factor analysis fits this book's objectives: determining the type of soft information that benefits lenders, as well as the types of soft information that increase loans' performance and decrease bad loan ratios. Nearly all questionnaire survey respondents (95%) belong to credit analysis or loan departments, and are not loan officers on the front lines in the customer service field. Loan officers,[4] who collect and process soft information, did not answer the survey questions, and thus, the questionnaire's answers represent the entire organization's stance on using soft information.

In conducting a factor analysis, the authors first determine a cutoff for the number of generated factors with an eigenvalue of ≥ 1, according to a combination of the Kaiser-Guttman rule and Cattell's screen criterion rule.[5] The authors then extracted the three underlying factors in line with these rules: (1) organizational systems, (2) business and management leadership, and (3) networks or alliances/partnerships.

Second, the authors used a varimax rotation to compute the factor loading, or the relationship of each questionnaire item from the SME Support, Japan survey to the corresponding communality. The varimax rotation is a method to select the rotation that best maximizes factor loadings; specifically, it is an orthogonal rotation technique that applies a principal component analysis to the factor loadings. Additionally, some loadings were so low that the authors considered that item as unassociated with the factor, and excluded items with loadings of less than 0.40. Factor loadings can be interpreted as standardized regression coefficients, as illustrated in the second to fourth columns in Table 3.1. The personnel evaluation system item in the second column has a correlation of 0.868 with Factor 1.

Loadings will vary even among items with reasonably high loadings. The authors reflect each item's unequal association with the factor using the regression method, a process to estimate factor score coefficients. A factor loading or a factor score is each item's weight in producing a score to represent the factor, and is obtained by multiplying a factor score coefficient with its respective standardized original item and summing these products.[6]

---

[4]The loan officer counsels the borrower, collects all pertinent information from the borrower and business environment surrounding its industry, and analyzes and verifies all information on the borrower's loan application.

[5]Appendix 3.2 describes the benefits of the combination of these rules.

[6]The regression model can accept biased estimations of the regression coefficients for the sake of decreasing variability. Thus, this model estimates biased factor scores (Kosfeld and Lauridsen 2008). This book also estimates factor scores using Bartlett's method, which produces factor scores with a mean of zero and a variance equal to the squared multiple correlation between the estimated and true factor values. The scores may correlate even when the factors are orthogonal. The result of estimated factor scores conforming to the Bartlett model is essentially the same as what conforms to the regression model. This consequently ensures the robustness of this book's results.

The authors then test whether each item within a single factor highly correlates by performing a maximum likelihood confirmatory factor analysis. The results reveal that the underlying three factors explain 67.82% of the total variance, with eigenvalues of 6.973, 2.709, and 1.227, respectively, and an average commonality of 0.460. These figures indicate that each item within a single factor could be singularly influential. To further test the extent to which the three factors are distinct and uncorrelated, the authors examine the pattern matrix to find no cross-loadings exist, as no item cross-loaded on another factor at a level higher than 0.40. This demonstrates that the three factors could have distinct constructs. Table 3.1 illustrates the factor analysis' results, including: the three underlying factors' loadings, the mean value and standard deviation from the original five-point Likert scale, and the original category label from the survey for each questionnaire item with loadings greater than or equal to 0.40. Appendix 3.2 details how to determine a cut-off for the number of the generated factors and includes a scree plot.

3.5 Univariate Tests: The Relationship Between Soft Information Factor Scores and a Bank's Performance

This chapter conducts univariate analyses in advance of the multivariate analyses in the next chapter, which more thoroughly includes all possible micro- and macro-control variables. The authors crossed loan profitability and bad loan ratios with two levels of soft information usage (high and low). A loan's profitability is the ratio of loan interest income to total assets, and a bad loan ratio is the ratio of bad loans to total assets. Japan has required the latter to be disclosed in accordance with the Financial Reconstruction Law, together with total loans. The authors' univariate analysis first divided latent factors into two groups, and conducted a *t*-test to determine the difference between the means of the high- versus low-scoring groups (see the left side of Table 3.2). Scores in this dichotomy were assigned to the high-scoring group if they surpassed the median, and to the low-scoring group if they were below the median. The authors also divided the factors into three groups to compare the top and bottom terciles; the analysis disregarded the middle tercile (see the right side of Table 3.2). Further, Table 3.2 summarizes the mean values and the *t*-test results regarding the differences between the means of the highest- versus lowest-tercile groups.

The authors' Hypothesis 2.1 predicted higher profitability when lenders use more soft information in their credit decisions. Specifically, the authors found that a higher usage of networks or alliances/partnerships contributes to greater loan profitability, consistent with Hypothesis 2.1. Regarding the networks or alliances/partnerships factor, the result indicates that the mean value of a high-factor group is greater than that of a low-factor group at the 1% significance level (two-tailed test) in both the dichotomized and tercile categories. No significant differences were found between the high- and low-scoring groups for the other two latent factors: organizational systems and business and management leadership factors. Regarding loan profitability as

Table 3.2 Univariate analysis: loan performance as a function of the soft information usage level

High versus Low (Dichotomized Groups)							High versus Low (Tercile Groups)						
***Panel A* organizational systems**							***Panel A* organizational systems**						
	High factor score	Low factor score	Difference	Ho: μ_1-$\mu_2 = 0$				High factor score	Low factor score	Difference	Ho: μ_1-$\mu_2 = 0$		
	μ_1	μ_2	μ_1-μ_2	Ha: μ_1-$\mu_2 \neq 0$	Ha: μ_1-$\mu_2 > 0$	Ha: μ_1-$\mu_2 < 0$		μ_1	μ_2	μ_1-μ_2	Ha: μ_1-$\mu_2 \neq 0$	Ha: μ_1-$\mu_2 > 0$	Ha: μ_1-$\mu_2 < 0$
				p-value							*p*-value		
Loan profitability	1.4011	1.4232	−0.0221	0.5787	0.7106	0.2894	Loan profitability	1.3898	1.4477	−0.0579	0.2040	0.898	0.1020
Bad loan ratio	7.2258	6.8751	0.3507	0.3738	0.1869	0.8131	Bad loan ratio	7.6528	6.9339	0.7189	0.1046	0.0523*	0.9477
No. of observations	154	153					No. of observations	123	109				
***Panel B* networks**							***Panel B* networks**						
	High factor score	Low factor score	Difference	Ho: μ_1-$\mu_2 = 0$				High factor score	Low factor score	Difference	Ho: μ_1-$\mu_2 = 0$		
	μ_1	μ_2	μ_1-μ_2	Ha: μ_1-$\mu_2 \neq 0$	Ha: μ_1-$\mu_2 > 0$	Ha: μ_1-$\mu_2 < 0$		μ_1	μ_2	μ_1-μ_2	Ha: μ_1-$\mu_2 \neq 0$	Ha: μ_1-$\mu_2 > 0$	Ha: μ_1-$\mu_2 < 0$
				p -value							*p* -value		
Loan profitability	1.4717	1.3522	0.1195	0.0025***	0.0012***	0.9988	Loan profitability	1.4772	1.3493	0.1279	0.0048***	0.0024***	0.9976

(continued)

Table 3.2 (continued)

Panel B networks						
Bad loan ratio	6.5157	7.5899	−1.0742	0.0062***	0.9969	0.0031***
No. of observations	154	153				
Panel C **business and leadership**						
	High factor score	Low factor score	Difference	Ho: $\mu_1-\mu_2=0$		
	μ_1	μ_2	$\mu_1-\mu_2$	Ha: $\mu_1-\mu_2 \neq 0$	Ha: $\mu_1-\mu_2 > 0$	Ha: $\mu_1-\mu_2 < 0$
				p-value		
Loan profitability	1.4015	1.4228	−0.0212	0.5937	0.7031	0.2969
Bad loan ratio	6.9445	7.1582	−0.2137	0.5882	0.7059	0.2941
No. of observations	154	153				

Panel B networks						
Bad loan ratio	6.6368	7.8942	−1.2575	0.0064***	0.9968	0.0032***
No. of observations	123	109				
Panel C **business and leadership**						
	High Factor Score	Low factor score	Difference	Ho: $\mu_1-\mu_2=0$		
	μ_1	μ_2	$\mu_1-\mu_2$	Ha: $\mu_1-\mu_2 \neq 0$	Ha: $\mu_1-\mu_2 > 0$	Ha: $\mu_1-\mu_2 < 0$
				p-value		
Loan profitability	1.3967	1.3906	0.0061	0.8963	0.4481	0.5519
Bad loan ratio	7.1489	7.3305	−0.1815	0.7029	0.6486	0.3514
No. of observations	123	109				

Notes Section 3.3 provides definitions of the three latent factors. Regarding definitions of loan performance, loan profitability is the ratio of interest income from loans to total assets, while the bad loan ratio is the ratio of bad loans to total loans. ***, **, and * indicate statistical significance at the 1%, 5%, and 10% levels, respectively

a function of the organizational systems factor's level of use, the high-scoring group's mean value was smaller—but not significantly so—than that in the low-scoring group in both the dichotomized and tercile analyses. Regarding loan profitability as a function of the business and management leadership factor's level of use, the high-scoring group's mean value was smaller—but not significantly so—than that in the low-scoring group in the dichotomized analysis, while the highest-tercile group's mean value was greater—but not significantly so—than that in the lowest-tercile group in the tercile analysis, consistent with the hypothesis in the tercile analysis in particular.

The authors' Hypothesis 2.5 predicted a lower bad loan ratio when lenders utilized more soft information in their credit decisions. Regarding bad loan ratios as a function of the networks or alliances/partnerships factor's level of use, the high-scoring group's mean value was significantly smaller than that of the low-scoring group at the 1% significance level (two-tailed test) in both the dichotomized and tercile categories, which is consistent with the hypothesis. Regarding the mean values for the bad loan ratio as a function of the business and leadership factor's level of use, the high-scoring group exhibited smaller values, although not significantly so, than that of the low-scoring group in both the dichotomized and tercile categories. Thus, the data trend can be said to be consistent with this hypothesis. With regard to a bad loan ratio as a function of the organizational systems factor's level of use, the mean value of the high-scoring group was higher, but not significantly so, than that of the low-scoring group in both the dichotomized and tercile categories, contrary to this hypothesis.

The authors then crossed loan profitability and bad loan ratios with two levels of The Herfindahl-Hirschman index (HHI), high and low. The HHI commonly measures the market concentration used to determine market competitiveness, and is calculated by squaring the market share from each lender competing in a local market then summing the resulting numbers. Therefore, the closer a market is to a monopoly, the more closely the HHI approaches 100%. The authors calculate the HHI by using the bank branch network's share of the local credit market—the ratio of each bank's number of administrative divisions to the total number of administrative divisions of all financial institutions in each prefecture throughout Japan.

The authors' univariate analysis first divided the indexes into two groups, and conducted a *t*-test to determine the difference between the means of the high- versus low-competition groups (see Panel A of Table 3.3). Indexes in this dichotomy were assigned to the high-competition group if they were below the median, and the low-competition group if they surpassed the median. The authors also divided the indexes into three groups, and compared the top and bottom terciles while disregarding the middle tercile in their analysis (see Panel B of Table 3.3). Further, Table 3.3 summarizes the mean values and the *t*-test results for the differences between the means of the high- versus low-competition groups.

The authors' Hypothesis 2.2 predicted lower profitability when lenders face severe interbank competition. The authors found that more severe competition deteriorates loan profitability, consistent with Hypothesis 2.2. The mean value of the high-competition group is less than that of the low-competition group at the 1% significance level (two-tailed test) for both the dichotomized and tercile categories. In

Table 3.3 Univariate analysis: loan performance as a function of interbank competition

	High competition	Low competition	Difference	Ho: μ_1-$\mu_2 = 0$		
	μ_1	μ_2	$\mu_1 - \mu_2$	Ha: μ_1-$\mu_2 \neq 0$	Ha: μ_1-$\mu_2 > 0$	Ha: μ_1-$\mu_2 < 0$
				p-value		
Panel A high versus low competition (Dichotomized Groups)						
Loan profitability	1.3522	1.4732	−0.1209	0.0022***	0.9989	0.0011***
Bad loan ratio	6.2042	7.9146	−1.7104	0.0000***	1.0000	0.0000***
No. of observations	155	152				
Panel B high competition versus low competition (Tercile Groups)						
Loan profitability	1.3577	1.5694	−0.2116	0.0000***	1.0000	0.0000***
Bad loan ratio	5.7540	8.2643	−2.5103	0.0000***	1.0000	0.0000***
No. observations	116	108				

Notes Regarding definitions of loan performance, loan profitability is the ratio of interest income from loans to total assets, while the bad loan ratio is the ratio of bad loans to total loans. The authors define interbank competition using the Herfindahl-Hirschman index, which is calculated by the number of branches in local markets. ***, **, and * indicate statistical significance at the 1%, 5%, and 10% levels, respectively.

Hypothesis 2.6, the authors predicted a higher bad loan ratio when lenders face fierce interbank competition, although this prediction was not fully realized. In fact, the authors found that a *t*-test for the difference between the means exhibited opposite results: a bad loan ratio of the high-competition group is smaller than that of the low-competition group at the 1% significance level (two-tailed test) for both the dichotomized and tercile categories. The results suggest that the lenders that exploit monopolistic environments tend to undertake riskier lending practices, and are consequently saddled with a higher non-performing loan ratio. This result is consistent with the modern competition-stability perspective, in that banks with higher degrees of market power bear significantly more loan risk (Berger et al. 2009).

Additionally, the authors crossed the three latent factors with two levels of market competition (high and low) in Table 3.4. Panel A in Table 3.4 displays the results of the *t*-test to determine the difference between the means for the dichotomized categories. Panel B notes the results for the tercile categories. Table 3.4 also illustrates the results of the *t*-test for the difference between the mean values of 22 soft information items, which constitute three latent factors as described in Table 3.1.

Table 3.4 Univariate analysis: the soft information usage level as a function of interbank competition

	High competition	Low competition	Ho: μ_1-$\mu_2 = 0$		
	$\mu 1$	$\mu 2$	Ha: μ_1-$\mu_2 \neq 0$	Ha: μ_1-$\mu_2 > 0$	Ha: μ_1-$\mu_2 < 0$
			p -value		
Panel A High versus low competition (Dichotomized Groups)					
Organizational systems					
Incentive system	2.742	2.815	0.275	0.863	0.137
Employee knowledge	3.271	3.199	0.308	0.154	0.846
Efficient labor–management relations	3.135	3.066	0.305	0.152	0.848
Company-specific improvement reporting system	2.852	2.868	0.799	0.400	0.601
Personnel evaluation system	2.794	2.801	0.901	0.549	0.451
Enhancement level of corporate education	3.000	3.000	1.000	0.500	0.500
IT system equipment	3.058	3.040	0.774	0.387	0.613
Factor Score	- 0.017	0.023	0.713	0.643	0.357
Networks					
Management with industrial experience	3.381	3.318	0.352	0.176	0.824
Managers' seniority	3.413	3.371	0.519	0.260	0.740
Managers' networks	3.284	3.278	0.928	0.464	0.536
Customer status	3.742	3.609	0.052*	0.026**	0.974
Supplier status	3.516	3.417	0.139	0.070*	0.931
Customer relationships	3.426	3.470	0.510	0.745	0.255

(continued)

Table 3.4 (continued)

	High competition	Low competition	Ho: μ_1-$\mu_2 = 0$		
	$\mu 1$	$\mu 2$	Ha: μ_1-$\mu_2 \neq 0$	Ha: μ_1-$\mu_2 > 0$	Ha: μ_1-$\mu_2 < 0$
			p -value		
Panel A High versus low competition (Dichotomized Groups)					
Supplier relationships	3.329	3.358	0.640	0.680	0.320
Factor Score	0.036	−0.010	0.658	0.329	0.671
Business and leadership					
Management capability	3.942	3.914	0.670	0.335	0.665
Management leadership	3.355	3.384	0.637	0.682	0.318
Managers' personality traits	3.516	3.477	0.554	0.277	0.723
Managerial succession	4.039	3.927	0.074*	0.037**	0.963
Technological superiority	3.845	3.934	0.164	0.918	0.082*
Advantage in the core business	3.923	3.854	0.308	0.154	0.846
Management philosophy	3.497	3.490	0.919	0.459	0.541
Business plan	3.961	3.993	0.636	0.682	0.318
Factor Score	0.060	−0.059	0.228	0.114	0.886
No. of observations	155	151			
Panel B high versus low competition (Tercile Groups)					
Organizational systems					
Incentive system	2.733	2.879	0.071*	0.964	0.036**
Employee knowledge	3.317	3.271	0.590	0.295	0.705

(continued)

Table 3.4 (continued)

Panel B high versus low competition (Tercile Groups)					
Efficient of labor–management relations	3.139	3.093	0.575	0.287	0.713
Company-specific improvement reporting system	2.881	2.907	0.747	0.627	0.373
Personnel evaluation system	2.802	2.841	0.614	0.693	0.307
Enhancement level of corporate education	2.960	3.037	0.312	0.844	0.156
IT system equipment	3.069	3.103	0.661	0.669	0.331
Factor score	−0.009	0.124	0.318	0.841	0.159
Networks					
Management with industrial experience	3.406	3.327	0.363	0.181	0.819
Managers' seniority	3.436	3.402	0.673	0.337	0.663
Managers' networks	3.238	3.299	0.423	0.788	0.212
Customer status	3.782	3.598	0.025**	0.012**	0.988
Supplier status	3.515	3.402	0.161	0.080*	0.920
Customer relationships	3.406	3.430	0.771	0.614	0.386
Supplier relationship	3.287	3.364	0.292	0.854	0.146
Factor score	0.000	−0.035	0.783	0.392	0.608
Business and leadership					
Management capability	3.990	3.907	0.310	0.155	0.845
Management leadership	3.406	3.402	0.958	0.479	0.521

(continued)

Table 3.4 (continued)

Panel B high versus low competition (Tercile Groups)					
Managers' personality traits	3.525	3.477	0.558	0.279	0.721
Managerial succession	4.059	3.944	0.116	0.058*	0.942
Technological superiority	3.891	3.972	0.284	0.858	0.142
Advantage in the core business	3.921	3.888	0.675	0.338	0.662
Management philosophy	3.505	3.523	0.820	0.590	0.410
Business plan	3.901	3.972	0.400	0.800	0.200
Factor score	0.113	−0.039	0.190	0.095*	0.905
No. of observations	101	107			

Notes The authors selected 22 soft information items strongly associated with the underlying latent factors, with factor loadings of greater than 0.4 (see Table 3.1). Regarding the definition of interbank competition measure, the authors use the Herfindahl-Hirschman index, which is calculated by the number of branches in local markets. ***, **, and * correspond to statistical significance at the 1%, 5%, and 10% levels, respectively.

The authors' Hypothesis 2.3 predicted a higher usage of soft information when lenders faced more severe interbank competition. On one hand, and regarding the networks or alliances/partnerships and business and leadership factors, the authors found that the usage level is greater, but not significantly so, for high competition than for low competition, and data trends are consistent with this hypothesis. On the other hand, the authors' *t*-test for the difference between the means exhibits opposite results for the organizational systems factor with a smaller usage level, although not significantly so, under high competition than under low competition. Subsequently, the data trends can be said to contradict this hypothesis.

3.6 Conclusions

This chapter first described the characteristics of Japanese financial institutions, with a specific focus on regional, second-tier regional, and shinkin banks, which construct a sample for analysis. Regional and second-tier regional banks are regulated under the Banking Act, and operate within each of Japan's 47 prefectures. These two types of regional banks are typically headquartered in the prefectural capital, conduct a majority of their business within a given prefecture, and provide an important source of credit to SMEs in Japan. On the other hand, shinkin banks are depository institutions and form regional financial cooperatives based on non-profit and mutual-aid membership schemes in compliance with the Shinkin Bank Act. Although shinkin banks limit their lending, in principle, to members, their functions in practice are nearly the same as of regional banks.

Second, this chapter presented the extent to which regional banks use soft information in their lending decisions. On average, Japanese small and medium-sized/regional financial institutions utilize soft information at a medium level in all three loan application phases: credit ratings, the assessment of borrowers and loan determinations, and in monitoring policies. Third, this chapter indicated the extent to which soft information impacts lenders' credit conditions. Generally, assessments of soft information are reflected in a variety of credit conditions, such as the amount offered, the interest rate, collateral amounts, and the duration of financing.

Fourth, the chapter extracted soft information factors from a 2008 questionnaire conducted by SME Support, Japan. This article most characteristically analyzes the influence of latent soft information factors on lender performance; it is also one of the first studies to use questionnaire survey data from lender representatives. The authors extracted three latent soft information factors in this chapter: organizational systems, business and management leadership, and networks or alliances/partnerships. The next chapter will execute multivariate analyses using these three latent factors.

Finally, this chapter conducted preliminary univariate analyses to investigate the relationship between soft information factor scores and banks' performance. The results reveal that the networks or alliances/partnerships factor positively correlates with loan profitability and negatively correlates with bad loan ratios, results consistent with the hypotheses developed in Chap. 2.

Appendix 3.1: Survey Questionnaire Items (Conducted by SME Support, Japan)

The survey was conducted in 2008 by the "Working Group on Intellectual Asset-Based Finance for Small and Medium-Sized Enterprises" under the "Study Group on Intellectual Asset-Based Management for Small and Medium-Sized Enterprises" at the Organization for Small and Medium Enterprises and Regional Innovation, Japan (SME Support, Japan). The questionnaire comprised 13 financial items and 54 non-financial items.

The 54 non-financial items were categorized into 7 groups, as follows: (1) human capital (top management); (2) external business environments; (3) business content; (4) customers and suppliers; (5) human capital (employees); (6) foundations of management, such as the management's philosophy, business model, and employee evaluation system; and (7) risk management and the corporate governance structure.

The authors labeled 38 characteristics as soft information, which has much in common with non-financial information, but by definition it focuses on unquantifiable, unverifiable, and sometimes subjective information (see Sect. 1.3) (Table 3.5).

Appendix 3.2: The Underlying Factors in the Factor Analysis

Although several heuristic rules can be used, this book extracts three underlying factors in conducting its factor analysis, in line with a combination of Kaiser-Guttman's rule and Cattell's screening criterion: (1) organizational systems, (2) business and management leadership, and (3) networks or alliances/partnerships. Combining these rules has the following benefits: practitioners can clearly select underlying factors with eigenvalues of ≥ 1; a factor with an eigenvalue of 1 accounts for as much variance as a single variable, and the factors that explain at least the same amount of variance as a single variable are worth retaining in the analysis.

Figure 3.4 provides a scree plot that illustrates eigenvalues on the y-axis and the number of factors on the x-axis. The point where the slope of the curve clearly levels off indicates the number of factors that the analysis should generate.

Table 3.5 The list of questionnaire items from the survey conducted by SME support, Japan

Number	Category	Questionnaire items	Information type
1	Financial items	Sales	Hard
2		Ordinary earnings	Hard
3		Amount of capital	Hard
4		Current ratio	Hard
5		Ratio of fixed assets to fixed liabilities	Hard
6		Capital to asset ratio	Hard
7		Cash flows	Hard
8		Capability of debt maturity	Hard
9		Capital to ordinary profit ratio	Hard
10		Sales to ordinary profit ratio	Hard
11		Inventory turnover periods	Hard
12		Sales growth	Hard
13		Earnings growth	Hard
14	Non-financial items: human capital (Top Management)	Management capability	Soft
15		Planning ability/the ability to create ideas	Soft
16		Leadership	Soft
17		Managers' personality traits	Soft
18		Managers' seniority	Hard
19		Management with industrial experience	Hard
20		History in managerial positions	Hard
21		Manager networks	Soft
22		Managerial succession	Soft
23		Health condition	Soft
24		Proprietor's individual assets	Hard
25		Degree of devotion to the business	Soft
26		External public relations activities	Soft
27	Non-financial items: external business environments	Industry share and position	Hard
28		Economic climate or sensitivity	Soft
29		Competitors' situation	Soft
30	Non-financial items: business content	Changes in business content	Soft
31		Superiority of techniques	Soft

(continued)

Table 3.5 (continued)

Number	Category	Questionnaire items	Information type
32		Intellectual property (Rights)	Hard
33		Superiority of brand products, goods, and services	Soft
34		Profitability of products, goods, and services	Soft
35		Advantage in the core business	Soft
36	Non-financial items: customers and suppliers	Customer status	Soft
37		Supplier status	Soft
38		Customer relations	Soft
39		Supplier relations	Soft
40		Customers' satisfaction level	Soft
41		Promotional/advertising activities	Soft
42	Non-financial items: credit history	Existence of a main bank	Hard
43		Status of transactions with other banks	Hard
44		Borrowing potential	Hard
45	Non-financial items: human capital (Employees)	Number of employees	Hard
46		Employees' average age and rate change from the previous year	Hard
47		Turnover ratio	Hard
48		Incentive system	Soft
49		Employee knowledge	Soft
50		Those with qualifications and techniques	Hard
51	Non-financial items: foundations of management	Management principles	Soft
52		Business plan	Soft
53		Company brand	Soft
54		Business model	Soft
55		Number of business offices	Hard
56		Efficient labor–management relations	Soft
57		Company-specific improvement reporting system/the number of improvements	Hard
58		Personnel evaluation system	Soft

(continued)

Table 3.5 (continued)

Number	Category	Questionnaire items	Information type
59		Degree of educational development	Soft
60		IT system equipment	Soft
61		The company's structure	Soft
62		Commitment to research and development	Soft
63		Support from the parent company	Soft
64		Related companies	Hard
65	Non-financial items: operational risk management	Response to leakage risk/operational confidentiality	Soft
66		Response to legal risk	Soft
67		Compliance system	Soft

Note The survey asked banks to respond regarding each item's level of use in lending decisions using a five-point Likert scale, ranging from one ("no use") to five ("considerable use").

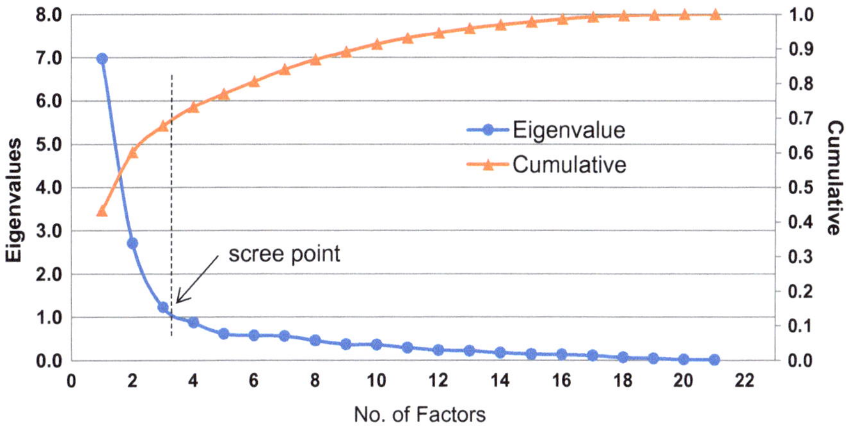

Fig. 3.4 The scree plot in the factor analysis

References

Bank of Japan (1998). The new foreign exchange and foreign trade law and Japan's balance of payments. In: *11th Meeting of the IMF Committee on Balance of Payments Statistics, Washington, D.C.* Retrieved October 21–23, from https://www.imf.org/external/bopage/pdf/121.pdf.

Berger, A. N., Klapper, L. F., & Turk-Ariss, R. (2009). Bank competition and financial stability. *Journal of Financial Services Research, 35*(2), 99–118.

Berger, A. N., & Udell, G. F. (1995). Relationship lending and lines of credit in small firm finance. *Journal of Business, 68*(3), 351–381.

Fukao, M. (1990). Liberalization of Japan's foreign exchange controls and structural changes in the balance of payments. *Bank of Japan Monetary and Economic Studies, 8*(2), 101–165.

Horiuchi, A. (1996). An evaluation of Japanese financial liberalization: A case study of corporate bond markets. *Financial Deregulation and Integration in East Asia, NBER-EASE, 5,* 167–192.

Kano, M., & Tsutsui, Y. (2003). Geographical segmentation in Japanese bank loan markets. *Regional Science and Urban Economics, 33*(2), 157–174.

Kosfeld, R., & Lauridsen, J. (2008). Factor analysis regression. *Statistical Papers, 49*(4), 653–667.

Liu, H., & Wilson, J. O. (2013). Competition and risk in Japanese banking. *The European Journal of Finance, 19,* 1–18.

Mabuchi, M. (1993). Deregulation and legalization of finanical policy. In G. Allinson & Y. Sone (Eds.), *Political dynamics in contemporary Japan*. Ithaca: Cornell University Press.

Ogura, Y., & Uchida, H. (2014). Bank consolidation and soft information acquisition in small business lending. *Journal of Financial Services Research, 45*(2), 173–200.

Osugi, K. (1990). Japan's experience of financial deregulation since 1984 in an international perspective. *BIS Economic Papers, 26*. Bank for International Settlements, Monetary and Economic Department. Retrieved from https://www.bis.org/publ/econ26.pdf.

Petersen, M. A., & Rajan, R. G. (1994). The benefits of lending relationships: Evidence from small business data. *The Journal of Finance, 49*(1), 3–37.

Schaede, U. (2005). The 'Middle-Risk Gap'and financial system reform: Small-firm financing in Japan. *Monetary and Economic Studies, 23*(1), 149–174.

Scott, J. A. (2004). Small business and the value of community financial institutions. *Journal of Financial Services Research, 25*(2), 207–230.

Uchida, H. (2011). What do banks evaluate when they screen borrowers? Soft information, hard information and collateral. *Journal of Financial Services Research, 40*(1–2), 29–48.

Uchida, H., Udell, G. F., & Watanabe, W. (2008). Bank size and lending relationships in Japan. *Journal of the Japanese and international Economies, 22*(2), 242–267.

Yoshimoto, K. (2013). Trancing the number of Japanese banks from the viewpoint of bank types(Suji wo ou gyotaibetsu no ginkosu, in Japanese). *Research Forcus*. The Japan Research Institute, Limited. Retrieved from https://www.jri.co.jp/MediaLibrary/file/report/researchfocus/pdf/6872.pdf.

Chapter 4
The Influence of Using Soft Information on Lender Performance in Competitive Local Markets: An Empirical Analysis

Abstract This chapter uses data from a survey conducted by the Organization for Small and Medium Enterprises and Regional Innovation, Japan (SME Support, Japan) to explore soft information factors' effects upon lender performance in competitive regional markets, especially as it concerns small and medium-sized/regional financial institutions. In the previous chapter, the authors extracted three latent factors: organizational systems, networks or alliances/partnerships, and business and management leadership. This chapter explores which type of soft information factor that impacts lender performance—profitability and bad loan ratios in particular—by multivariate analyses; and also determines how any combination of soft information factors contributes to lender performance. Further, this chapter investigates soft information factors' potent influence on lender performance in the face of interbank competition. The authors' multivariate models include all the possible control variables that might influence lender performance, including bank- and locally specific variables. Finally, this chapter conducts robustness tests to evaluate the multivariate models' analytical quality.

Keywords Soft information · Loan profitability · Bad loan ratio · Interbank competition · Organizational system · Networks or alliances/partnerships · Business and leadership

4.1 Multivariate Regression Models

This chapter empirically tests whether using soft information factors in lending decisions significantly improves lender performance, specifically in a competitive local market. This study's research design involves a multivariate cross-sectional regression analysis using 2008 survey data from SME Support, Japan. This type of regression analysis is used because the dependent variable—the lender's performance—is affected by a variety of micro- and macro-environments, such as the market, legislation, and society. The estimation is based on a sample of 307 small and medium-sized/regional financial institutions that participated in the questionnaire survey, with a response rate of 78.5%.

T. Yosano and T. Nakaoka, *Utilization of Soft Information on Bank Performance*, Development Bank of Japan Research Series,
https://doi.org/10.1007/978-981-13-8472-1_4

To address the measurement error problem in using multiple regressions, this study employs additional tests: the *F*-test and random effects generalized least squares (GLS) regressions, which will be further discussed in Sect. 4.4. The latter regressions assess the estimates of the multivariate analyses' parameters, as these are insensitive to the exact specifications used in the multiple regressions. Additionally, Sect. 4.4 uses raw values from each questionnaire item to assess each of the estimated factor scores' validity.

The following cross-sectional regression model is used to test the hypothesized relationships between a lender's performance and each soft information factor's level of use in local competitive markets, as described in Hypotheses 1–7:

$$\begin{aligned} Performance_i = & f\,(Soft\ Information\ Factors_i,\ Interbank\ Competition_i,\\ & Bank\text{-}Specific\ Characteristics_i,\\ & Local\ Market\text{-}Specific\ Characteristics_{i,j},\ \varepsilon_i). \end{aligned}$$

The authors' multivariate analysis assumes that lenders' loan performance is a function of soft information use, interbank competition, bank-specific variables, and local market-specific dvariables. Bank-specific variables denote an individual bank's specific characteristics, excluding soft information factors and the Herfindahl-Hirschman Index (HHI), which measures interbank competition. Local market-specific variables denote regional specific characteristics, which are the common attributes among banks headquartered in the same local prefecture. The subscript *i* denotes an individual bank, and *j* denotes the prefectural market.[1,2]

[1]This book's regression model involves multiple independent variables, and thus, the authors calculated the variance inflation factor (VIF) to ascertain whether the regression model has a multi-collinearity problem. This phenomenon involves one predictor variable that can be linearly and substantially predicted from the other variables in the multivariate regression. If a multi-collinearity problem arises, the multiple regression model's coefficient estimates may change erratically in response to small changes in the model or the data. The VIF quantifies the multi-collinearity's severity in an ordinary least squares regression analysis. Unfortunately, several rules associated with VIF are regarded as a sign of severe or serious multi-collinearity, but the "rule of 10" is the most common (O'Brien 2007). When the VIF exceeds 10, the rule of 10 is interpreted as casting doubt on the regression results. In this chapter's regression models, all the independent variables' VIFs were less than 7, which is acceptable in accord with the rule of 10. Consequently, the authors concluded that none of the regression models exhibit a severe multi-collinearity problem.

[2]The authors' multivariate models involve all control variables that might influence banks' loan performance to exclude the possibility of covariation between the dependent and missing control variables. This ensures unbiased and consistent estimates in the regression.

4.2 Dependent and Explanatory Variables

Prior researchers have rarely examined the relationship between soft information utilization and loan performance. Therefore, the authors control for all variables that might influence loan performance to exclude the possibility of covariation between the dependent variables and the missing control variables in the multivariate regression analysis. In addition to defining the dependent variables, the authors subsequently describe the definitions of independent variables as follows: soft information factors extracted using the factor analysis of survey data, bank-specific variables, and local market-specific variables. Table 4.1 details the variable definitions.

4.2.1 Soft Information Factors

Organizational systems. The *organizational systems* factor is comprised of seven soft information items (Cronbach's alpha = 0.878). These systems involve not only the process and rules that govern both the measures and performance used to evaluate employees' actions, but also the rewards and punishments imposed on those employees as a consequence of their misdemeanor (Jensen and Meckling 1996). The organizational systems factor consists of three subfactors. The first subfactor involves the human resource management system, the questionnaire items for which are comprised of a personnel evaluation system (0.868), a company-specific improvement reporting system (0.819), and an incentive system (0.718). The second subfactor is the management system's effectiveness; its questionnaire items include the enhancement level of corporate education (0.674), employee knowledge (0.535), and efficient labor–management relations (0.611). The third subfactor involves IT system equipment (0.640).

Networks or alliances/partnerships. Similarly, the *networks or alliances/partnerships* factor is comprised of seven items (Cronbach's alpha = 0.860). The networks or alliances/partnerships factor is defined as any collection of actors that pursue repeated, enduring exchange relationships with one another (Podolny and Page 1998). This factor consists of two subfactors. First, the network subfactor has questionnaire items comprised of supplier relationships (0.807), customer relationships (0.727), supplier status (0.706), and customer status (0.623). Second, industrial knowledge assets are comprised of such questionnaire items as managers' seniority (0.506), management with industrial experience (0.497), and manager networks (0.456). A firm's set of both horizontal and vertical relationships with other organizations include tightly woven networks, whether with suppliers, customers, competitors, or other entities—including relationships across industries (Gulati et al. 2000; Inkpen and Tsang 2005). Additionally, industrial knowledge assets are a source of lenders' competitive advantage, which flows from the creation, ownership, protection, and use of difficult-to-imitate commercial and

Table 4.1 Variable descriptions

Symbol	Description	Source
Dependent variables		
Loan profitability$_i$	The ratio of interest income from loans and discounts to total assets of bank *i* in the year 2007	Nikkei
Bad loan ratio$_i$	The ratio of bad loans to total assets of bank *i* at the end of 2007. The bad loans are Problem loans consist of four types of loans: bankrupt, quasi-bankrupt, doubtful, and substandard loans under the Financial Reconstruction Law	Nikkei
Independent variables		
Bank variables		
Organizational systems$_i$	The organizational system is one of three principal factors based on the factor analysis for each of the soft information items, and is a factor score for bank *i*. Soft information items are surveyed asking about degree of use in credit decision making by five Likert-type scale (1 = "Do not use at all," 5 = "Considerably use") in 2007	Survey data
Networks$_i$	The networks or alliances/partnerships factor is one of three principal factors based on the factor analysis for each of the soft information items, and is the factor score of bank *i* in 2007	Survey data
Business and leadership$_i$	The business and management leadership factor is one of three principal factors based on the factor analysis for each of the soft information items, and is the factor score of bank *i* in 2007	Survey data
Bank size$_i$	Total assets of bank *i* at the end of 2007	Nikkei
Growth$_i$	The total assets growth of bank *i* from 2006 to 2007	Nikkei
Branch ratio$_i$	The ratio of branches to total assets for bank *i* at the end of 2007 $\times 10^4$	Nikkei
SME lending ratio$_i$	The ratio of SME lending to total lending from bank *i* at the end of 2007	Annual reports
Capital$_i$	The ratio of net assets to total assets of bank *i* at the end of 2007	Nikkei
Local share$_i$	Banks' local market share is based on their share of loans in the local market from bank *i* at the end of 2007	FM
Soft collecting (D)	Dummy variable that equals one if bank *i* has a hearing sheet of soft information	Survey data
Shinkin (D)	Dummy variable that equals one if bank *i* is a Shinkin bank	Annual reports
Mergers and HC (D)	Dummy variable that equals one if bank *i* has experienced a merger or established a bank holding company between 2003 and 2007	Annual reports

(continued)

Table 4.1 (continued)

Symbol	Description	Source
Local market variables		
Herfindahl_{ij}	The Herfindahl-Hirschman index is based on the number of branches bank *i* has in the local market *j*	DJFI
Land price_{ij}	The growth rate of land prices in local market *j* is the log differences for land prices between 2005 and 2006, based on the location of bank *i*	LPS
Job offers_{ij}	The effective ratio of (seasonally adjusted) job offers to applicants in local market *j*, based on bank *i* locations in 2006	LS
Number of firms	The number of firms in local market *j*, based on bank *i* locations in 2006	SAR
Urban (D)	Dummy variable that equals one if bank *i* is headquartered in an area with a population of one million or more citizens	CD

Notes This table displays the description and sources of the dependent and independent variables. The (D) notation indicates a dummy variable. "Nikkei" stands for the Nikkei NEEDS-Financial QUEST database by Nikkei Media Marketing, Inc.; FM stands for Financial Map in Japan by the Japan Financial News Co. Ltd.; CD stands for "census data" from the Ministry of Internal Affairs and Communications; DJFI stands for the Directory of Japanese Financial Intermediations (CD-ROM version) by the Japan Financial News Co., Ltd.; LPS stands for the Land Price Survey by Prefectural Governments from the Ministry of Land Infrastructure, Transport and Tourism; LS stands for Labor Statistics by the Ministry of Health, Labor and Welfare; and SAR stands for the National Tax Agency's Statistical Annual Report.

industrial assets. Such assets include tacit and codified knowledge, both technical and organizational (Teece 2000).

Business and management leadership. Finally, the *business and management leadership* factor is comprised of eight measurement items (Cronbach's alpha = 0.801). Business and management leadership illustrates the business plan and managerial leadership, the latter of which enables the firm to pursue and implement the former. This factor consists of two subfactors: the business and management leadership subfactors. The questionnaire's items regarding the business subfactor include a business plan (0.569), any advantage in the core business (0.509), and technological superiority (0.461). This subfactor involves the company's business plan and internal assets and skills. The business plan enables the company to develop and implement an internally consistent set of objectives and functional policies that collectively define its market position (Porter 1991). Internal assets and skills are typified by the firm's core business and technologies (Radosevic 1999). The leadership subfactor is comprised of such questionnaire items as management capability (0.590), managers' personality traits (0.547), management leadership (0.501) and philosophy (0.496), and managerial succession (0.445). This subfactor can lead or direct the entire organization, while managerial leadership determines the firm's performance (Day and

Lord 1988), and is comprised of the three basic skills: generic, industry-related, and firm-specific. These managerial skills' coherence with the firm's business operations enable the firm to operate its business both effectively and efficiently (Castanias and Helfat 1991).

4.2.2 Loan Performance

Loan profitability. Regional banks' profitability in the lending operation can be assessed using multiple financial metrics, such as loan profitability, or the ratio of interest income from loans and discounts to total assets; the ratio of net interest income from loans and discounts to total assets; and return on assets (ROA). The authors' analysis adopted loan profitability, as this study aims to measure the performance of banks' credit operations. Therefore, the authors did not use an ROA metric as the numerator would involve revenue outside the lending operation. Net interest income is defined as the interest income from loans and discounts minus loan losses and any provision for possible loan losses. Many accounting researchers have noted that management often arbitrarily decides on a figure for the provision of possible loan losses, and therefore, the authors' analysis did not use net loan profitability.

Bad loan ratio. Regional banks' ability to utilize credit analyses can be measured by the bad loan ratio, or the ratio of bad loans to total assets. However, bad loans in Japan can be defined in several ways. One is "problem loans" (Mamatzakis et al. 2016). Problem loans consist of four types of loans: bankrupt, quasi-bankrupt, doubtful, and substandard loans under the Financial Reconstruction Law. These types of loans are classified as problem assets under the Financial Reconstruction Law. Another way to define bad loans involves risk-monitored loans, disclosed in accordance with the Banking Law. Risk-monitored loans consist of two types of loans: bankrupt loans and restructured loans. Bankrupt loans are loans to borrowers in legal bankruptcy and past due loans by 6 months or more. Restructured loans are named after the sum of past due loans by 3 months but less than 6 months and restructured loans. Accordingly, the authors used both bad loan definitions in their analysis, but reported only the results from the first, as the results from the second were nearly the same as the first.

All the data used to calculate loan profitability and the bad loans ratio were obtained through the Nikkei NEEDS-Financial QUEST database by Nikkei Media Marketing, Inc. All independent variables are measured in the 2007 accounting period, as this is the same period in which the survey was conducted.

4.2.3 Bank-Specific and Local Market-Specific Variables

The Herfindahl-Hirschman index. This book follows previous studies that argue the existence of bank branches—which can make banking franchises more valuable—creates a motivation for lenders to engage in relationship lending and to address potential competitive pressure on banks in local credit markets. Thus, the local market's number of bank branches was used to calculate the HHI (Berger et al. 2005; Degryse and Ongena 2005, 2007). A higher HHI indicates a greater bank monopoly in the local market.

According to the traditional competition-fragility perspective, higher competition encourages banks to assume higher risk, as this gives rise to diminishing monopolistic rents. In this scenario, riskier lending due to higher competition results in higher bad loan ratios. Alternatively, and according to the modern competition-stability perspective, a monopolistic environment encourages banks to assume higher risks, but riskier lending practices result in adverse selection and increase bad loan ratios. This suggests that monopolistic rents from low competition increase the bank's moral hazard (Berger et al. 2009). Subsequently, the authors determine the perspective that best accounts for the data by including a square term for the HHI in their analysis.

Bank size and growth. On one hand, substantial empirical evidence indicates that large banks record more profit than smaller ones (Stiroh and Rumble 2006). On the other hand, some empirical evidence also reveals opposite results (Carter et al. 2004). Therefore, the authors controlled for any potential extraneous effects of economies of scale and/or any potential differences in credit risk management techniques between the organizational size and its growth (*Bank Size*, *Growth*). The authors also include a square term for *Growth* to consider diseconomies of scale.

Branch ratio. The ratio of branches to total assets (*Branch Ratio*) was used due to its potential effect on regional networks. Franchised neighborhood bank offices in the local area strengthens the community's knowledge of those banks and improves the former's judgment in assessing loan applicants' creditworthiness. Banks expanding their market share by franchising their branches results in their improved ability to determine creditworthiness and reduces their risk of bankruptcy. This method is independent of any risk reduction obtained through a diverse lending portfolio (Berger et al. 2001; Bofondi and Gobbi 2006).

SME lending ratio. The ratio of SME lending to total lending (*SME Lending Ratio*) was used to control for higher interest rates in SME lending. The higher the SME lending ratio, the higher the interest rate for SME lending, as SME lending involves a greater risk than lending to larger businesses. Previous research has noted that community banks exploit the generating of rents from small business lending, and suggested that banks should focus on these loan types to survive in a competitive market (Carter et al. 2004; Carter and McNulty 2005).

Capital. The ratio of net assets to total assets (*Capital*) was used due to its potential function as a barrier and/or a buffer, while capital functions as not only an entry barrier for credit lending, but also a buffer when a bank decides to assume risk. Only banks with significant capital can assume such risks and extend credit in SME lending.

Local share. Banks' local market share is based on their share of loans in the local market. This index is used as a proxy variable representing the bank's familiarity with local market characteristics and its reputation in the local community (Bharath et al. 2007). The local share also represents monopolistic power (Bofondi and Gobbi 2006) as well as the previously described HHI.

Soft collecting (D). The soft collecting dummy variable indicates whether the lender uses a hearing sheet for soft information—which essentially judges borrowers' creditworthiness—in the credit screening or monitoring processes in their lending decisions. The 2008 SME Support, Japan, survey asked whether the lender uses such a hearing sheet.

Shinkin (D). The data sample used in this book involves regional banks, second-tier regional banks, and shinkin banks to control for the difference in organizational type. Jimènez and Saurina (2004) demonstrated that credit cooperatives, which do not have shareholders but do have owner/partners, assume more risk than banks. The dummy variable *Shinkin* indicates whether each bank is a shinkin bank.

Mergers and HC (D). This book's data sample includes regional banks that experienced mergers and acquisitions or business integration by establishing a holding company. This dummy variable is included to control for this effect.

Additionally, banks' performance and borrowers' default risk might systematically depend on local macro-economic circumstances. Therefore, the authors controlled for the following four regional economic characteristics:

Land price. The growth rate of land prices (*Land Price*) is linked to the lending property's collateral value. An increase in collateral value facilitates lending, as banks will be able to recover their principal if the firm faces bankruptcy. Land price also acts as a lagged indicator of the local economic climate.

Job offers. The number of job offers indicates an effective ratio of (seasonally adjusted) job offers to applicants in the local market. This also acts as an indicator of the local economic climate, as a sound economic environment leads to lenders' higher performance.

Number of firms. The number of firms is included to control for firms' potential financing needs. This indicates the local economic climate, as a large number of firms leads to better lender performance.

Urban (D). The dummy variable *Urban* indicates whether the lender is headquartered in an area with a population of one million or more citizens.

Table 4.1 describes all dependent and explanatory variables, with bank-specific explanatory variables and local market-specific variables displayed separately. The second column in this table displays variable definitions, while the last column notes the data source.

Table 4.2 notes descriptive statistics of the dependent and independent variables. As this book studies whether relationship lending contributes to regional financial institutions' performance, the authors incorporate loan profitability and bad loan ratios. Further, the authors sorted soft information factors in this book into three categories based on survey data illustrated in Chap. 3: organizational systems, networks or alliances/partnerships, and business and management leadership. The authors then normalized these three metrics, with a mean value for loan profitability and bad loan ratios of 1.412% and 7.051%, respectively.

4.3 Regression Results

4.3.1 *Multivariate Analysis of Loan Profitability*

The third to sixth columns from Panel A in Table 4.3 display the results of the three latent factors' influence on loan profitability. The authors' Hypothesis 2.1 predicted the three soft information factors—organizational systems, networks or alliances/partnerships, and business and leadership—would positively influence loan profitability. The authors' predictions were supported by two soft information factors: networks or alliances/partnerships, and business and leadership. On one hand, the full model's coefficient of the networks or alliances/partnerships factor is 0.0413, which is significant at the 1% level (*t*-statistic: 3.49), and that of the business and leadership factor is 0.0299, which is significant at the 5% level (*t*-statistic: 2.01). The absolute magnitude of the networks or alliances/partnerships factor is 38% greater than that of the business and management leadership factor.

On the other hand, the coefficient of the organizational systems factor was negative at −0.0219, and significant at the 10% level (*t*-statistic: −1.90). Contrary to the authors' Hypothesis 2.1, this result surprisingly supports the notion that lenders' excessive reliance on organizational systems hinders loan profitability; this information typifies the organization's appearance as a façade by which the firm advocates their assertiveness. An organization's outward appearance does not always denote better risk measures.

The seventh to ninth columns from Panel A in Table 4.3 illustrate the magnitudes of the latent factors' interaction effects on loan profitability. These results indicate that the interaction term between the organizational systems and business and leadership factors is positive at 0.0240, and significant at the 10% level (*t*-statistic: 1.83). Although the organizational systems factor exhibits a solitary negative effect at −0.0274, and is significant at the 5% level (*t*-statistic: −2.27), the simultaneous use of information on the business and management leadership factor eliminates the organizational systems factor's negative effect, and reverts loan profitability to its original level.

The authors' Hypothesis 2.2 predicted the HHI's positive impact on loan profitability. The results indicated in Panel A of Table 4.3 strongly support this hypothesis in all eight regression models. The HHI's coefficient in the full model is 1.2083, at the 1% significance level (*t*-statistic: 4.27). Appendix 4.1 reveals a positive linear relationship obtained by regressing loan profitability on the HHI, measured by the square of the number of branches, which has been adjusted for any covariation with other control variables in the full model.

Table 4.2 Descriptive statistics

Variables	Mean	S. D.	Min.	25th Pctile	Median	75th Pctile	Max.
Dependent variables							
Performance variables							
Loan profitability (%)	1.412	0.348	0.355	1.168	1.372	1.662	2.281
Bad loan ratio (%)	7.051	3.449	2.129	4.387	6.190	8.742	23.244
Independent variables							
Measures of soft information							
Organizational systems	0.003	0.949	−4.203	−0.181	0.245	0.413	2.242
Networks	0.012	0.900	−2.237	−0.669	−0.225	0.826	2.585
Business and leadership	−0.00003	0.861	−2.134	−0.571	0.013	0.485	2.622
Bank characteristics variables							
Bank size (million yen)	932,808	1,566,715	39,190	149,004	363,999	876,533	11,625,677
Growth (%)	1.988	6.542	−7.513	−0.182	1.141	2.777	65.612
Branch ratio	0.824	0.388	0.174	0.547	0.806	0.998	2.571
SME lending ratio (%)	87.686	8.564	58.959	82.954	89.972	93.865	99.983
Capital (%)	8.080	4.785	0.580	4.850	6.810	10.130	31.300
Local share (%)	6.549	10.483	0.042	1.010	2.111	5.700	48.300
Soft collecting (D) (1, 0)	0.534	0.500	0.000	0.000	1.000	1.000	1.000
Shinkin (D) (1,0)	0.760	0.428	0.000	1.000	1.000	1.000	1.000
Mergers and HC (D) (1, 0)	0.143	0.351	0.000	0.000	0.000	0.000	1.000
Regional characteristics variables							
Herfindahl	0.152	0.070	0.049	0.080	0.142	0.216	0.295
Land price (%)	1.511	7.076	−7.953	−3.572	−0.895	2.934	20.555
Job offers	1.095	0.358	0.430	0.890	1.070	1.300	2.020
Number of firms	10.859	0.995	9.216	9.965	10.654	11.686	13.272
Urban (D) (1, 0)	0.169	0.376	0.000	0.000	0.000	0.000	1.000
No. of observations	307						

Note Table 4.1 provides definitions of the dependent and independent variables.

Table 4.3 The effects of soft information and interbank competition on loan profitability

Panel A: Baseline model and interaction model—loan profitability								
Variables	Control variables	Single model			Full model	Interaction model		
	Coefficient (*t*-statistics)	Coefficient (*t*-statistics)			Coefficient (*t*-statistics)	Coefficient (*t*-statistics)		
Organizational systems (a)		−0.0193* (−1.65)			−0.0219* (−1.90)	−0.0244 ** (−2.13)	−0.0274** (−2.27)	−0.021* (−1.85)
Networks (b)			0.0437*** (3.63)		0.0413 *** (3.49)	0.0433 *** (3.53)	0.0394*** (3.38)	0.046*** (3.81)
Business and leadership (c)				0.0344** (2.30)	0.0299 ** (2.01)	0.0285* (1.93)	0.0321** (2.10)	0.0303** (2.07)
Organ. systems × networks						0.0207 (1.54)		
Organ. systems × Bus. and leader.							0.0240* (1.83)	
Networks × Bus. and leader.								−0.0192 (−1.63)
	***F*-statistics: (a) = (b) = (c) = 0**				***6.53****	***5.13****	***5.26****	***5.54****
Herfindahl	1.1361*** (3.97)	1.1763*** (4.09)	1.1284*** (4.01)	1.1749*** (4.12)	1.2083*** (4.27)	1.2114*** (4.26)	1.1905*** (4.17)	1.2109*** (4.29)

(continued)

Table 4.3 (continued)

Panel A: Baseline model and interaction model—loan profitability								
Variables	Control variables	Single model			Full model	Interaction model		
	Coefficient (*t*-statistics)	Coefficient (*t*-statistics)			Coefficient (*t*-statistics)	Coefficient (*t*-statistics)		
Log (bank size)	0.0032 (0.10)	0.0013 (0.04)	0.00013 (0.00)	0.0024 (0.07)	−0.0026 (−0.08)	−0.0028 (−0.09)	−0.00088 (−0.03)	−0.0011 (−0.03)
Growth	−0.0097* (−1.65)	−0.0094* (−1.59)	−0.0102* (−1.79)	−0.0102* (−1.75)	−0.0102* (−1.79)	−0.0103* (−1.79)	−0.0101* (−1.74)	−0.0104* (−1.83)
(Growth − Ave. growth)^2	0.000049 (0.37)	0.000045 (0.34)	0.000069 (0.53)	0.000062 (0.47)	0.000074 (0.57)	0.000076 (0.57)	0.000072 (0.54)	0.000080 (0.61)
Branch ratio	0.3165*** (3.44)	0.3166*** (3.47)	0.3141*** (3.62)	0.3266*** (3.71)	0.3231*** (3.90)	0.3232*** (3.93)	0.3234*** (4.00)	0.3341*** (3.93)
SME lending ratio	0.0143*** (5.76)	0.0144*** (5.79)	0.0142*** (5.85)	0.0139*** (5.64)	0.0140*** (5.79)	0.0138*** (5.71)	0.0137*** (5.66)	0.0139*** (5.77)
Capital	−0.0195*** (−6.35)	−0.0197*** (−6.44)	−0.0194*** (−6.58)	−0.0194*** (−6.23)	−0.0194*** (−6.57)	−0.0193*** (−6.53)	−0.0201*** (−6.70)	−0.0194*** (−6.53)
Local share	−0.00103 (−0.40)	−0.00089 (−0.34)	−0.00103 (−0.41)	−0.00102 (−0.40)	−0.00086 (−0.34)	−0.00102 (−0.41)	−0.00105 (−0.41)	−0.00068 (−0.27)
Soft collecting (D)	−0.0188 (−0.72)	−0.0174 (−0.67)	−0.0223 (−0.87)	−0.0256 (−0.97)	−0.0266 (−1.03)	−0.0262 (−1.02)	−0.0283 (−1.10)	−0.0243 (−0.95)
Shinkin (D)	−0.3976*** (−8.18)	−0.3962*** (−8.27)	−0.3847*** (−8.14)	−0.3981*** (−8.03)	−0.3843*** (−8.10)	−0.3847*** (−8.00)	−0.3781*** (−8.04)	−0.3819*** (−8.15)

(continued)

Table 4.3 (continued)

Panel A: Baseline model and interaction model—loan profitability								
Variables	Control variables	Single model			Full model	Interaction model		
	Coefficient (t-statistics)	Coefficient (t-statistics)			Coefficient (t-statistics)	Coefficient (t-statistics)		
Mergers and HC (D)	0.0100 (0.25)	0.0080 (0.21)	0.0103 (0.26)	0.0115 (0.30)	0.0093 (0.25)	0.0096 (0.26)	0.0037 (0.10)	0.0099 (0.26)
Land price	0.0019 (0.70)	0.0019 (0.73)	0.0026 (0.97)	0.0024 (0.88)	0.0030 (1.15)	0.0030 (1.15)	0.0028 (1.07)	0.0029 (1.10)
Job offers	−0.3257*** (−7.76)	−0.3219*** (−7.75)	−0.3271*** (7.91)	−0.3257*** (−7.75)	−0.3227*** (−7.90)	−0.3273*** (−7.95)	−0.3231*** (−7.92)	−0.3162*** (−7.70)
Log (number of firms)	0.0748*** (2.69)	0.0764*** (2.75)	0.0718*** (2.63)	0.0766*** (2.79)	0.0753*** (2.80)	0.0745*** (2.77)	0.0745*** (2.74)	0.0758*** (2.81)
Urban (D)	0.0966** (2.00)	0.0990** (2.08)	0.0862* (1.83)	0.0933** (1.99)	0.0866* (1.90)	0.0916** (2.01)	0.0922** (2.02)	0.0904** (1.99)
Const.	−0.2974 (−0.51)	−0.3097 (−0.53)	−0.2235 (−0.40)	−0.2848 (−0.50)	−0.2306 (−0.42)	−0.2014 (−0.37)	−0.2088 (−0.39)	−0.2670 (−0.48)
No. of observations	307	307	307	307	307	307	307	307
R-Square	0.627	0.630	0.639	0.634	0.647	0.649	0.651	0.650

(continued)

Table 4.3 (continued)

Panel B: Joint effects of soft information and competition—loan profitability					
Variables	Control variables	Single model			Full model
	Coefficient (t-statistics)	Coefficient (t-statistics)			Coefficient (t-statistics)
Organizational systems (a)		−0.0254* (−1.81)			−0.0284** (−2.00)
Organ. Systems × high comp (a)′		0.0160 (0.62)			0.0211 (0.83)
***F*-statistics: (a) = (a)′ = 0**		***1.77***			***2.09***
Networks (b)			0.0246* (1.82)		0.0249* (1.77)
Networks × high comp (b)′			0.0529* (1.86)		0.0543* (1.95)
***F*-statistics: (b) = (b)′ = 0**			***7.17******		***7.59******
Business and leadership (c)				0.0130 (0.74)	0.0091 (0.48)
Bus. and leader. × high comp (c)′				0.0571* (1.79)	0.0631** (2.03)
***F*-statistics: (c) = (c)′ = 0**				***3.78****	***4.36****
	***F*-statistics: (a) = (b) = (c) = 0**				***2.67****
	***F*-statistics: (a)′ = (b)′ = (c)′ = 0**				***2.36****

(continued)

Table 4.3 (continued)

Panel B: Joint effects of soft information and competition—loan profitability					
Variables	Control variables	Single model			Full model
	Coefficient (*t*-statistics)	Coefficient (*t*-statistics)			Coefficient (*t*-statistics)
Herfindahl	1.1361*** (3.97)	1.1820*** (4.11)	1.1177*** (3.97)	1.1497*** (4.06)	1.1761*** (4.19)
Log (bank size)	0.0032 (0.10)	0.0016 (0.05)	−0.0028 (−0.09)	−0.0048 (−0.15)	−0.0133 (−0.43)
Growth	−0.0097* (−1.65)	−0.0093 (−1.56)	−0.0104* (−1.84)	−0.0105* (−1.81)	−0.0108* (−1.89)
$(\text{Growth} - \text{Ave. growth})^2$	0.000049 (0.37)	0.000043 (0.32)	0.000071 (0.56)	0.000064 (0.49)	0.000079 (0.61)
Branch ratio	0.3165*** (3.44)	0.3179*** (3.48)	0.3088*** (3.50)	0.3186*** (3.51)	0.3113*** (3.59)
SME lending ratio	0.0143*** (5.76)	0.0143*** (5.76)	0.0142*** (5.83)	0.0141*** (5.58)	0.0141*** (5.68)
Capital	−0.0195*** (−6.35)	−0.0198*** (−6.37)	−0.0201*** (−6.86)	−0.0199*** (−6.36)	−0.0208*** (−6.99)
Local share	−0.00103 (−0.40)	−0.00086 (−0.34)	−0.00062 (−0.25)	−0.00030 (−0.11)	0.00037 (0.15)
Soft collecting (D)	−0.0188 (−0.72)	−0.0185 (−0.72)	−0.0215 (−0.85)	−0.0267 (−1.02)	−0.0293 (−1.18)
Shinkin (D)	−0.3976*** (−8.18)	−0.3950*** (−8.16)	−0.3817*** (−8.09)	−0.3949*** (−7.76)	−0.3752*** (−7.62)

(continued)

Table 4.3 (continued)

Panel B: Joint effects of soft information and competition—loan profitability					
Variables	Control variables	Single model			Full model
	Coefficient (*t*-statistics)	Coefficient (*t*-statistics)			Coefficient (*t*-statistics)
Mergers and HC (D)	0.0100 (0.25)	0.0065 (0.17)	0.0108 (0.27)	0.0167 (0.43)	0.0139 (0.35)
Land price	0.0019 (0.70)	0.0019 (0.72)	0.0026 (0.97)	0.0025 (0.92)	0.0032 (1.22)
Job offers	−0.3257*** (−7.76)	−0.3227*** (−7.73)	−0.3275*** (−7.92)	−0.3266*** (−7.81)	−0.3257*** (−7.99)
Log (number of firms)	0.0748*** (2.69)	0.0771*** (2.77)	0.0756*** (2.76)	0.0774*** (2.84)	0.0809*** (3.02)
Urban (D)	0.0966** (2.00)	0.0983** (2.07)	0.0642 (1.31)	0.0862* (1.86)	0.0541 (1.15)
Const.	−0.2974 (−0.51)	−0.3189 (−0.55)	−0.2149 (−0.38)	−0.2102 (−0.36)	−0.1438 (−0.26)
No. of observations	307	307	307	307	307
R-Square	0.627	0.630	0.643	0.638	0.658

Notes Table 4.1 provides definitions of the dependent and independent variables. ***, **, and * denote statistical significance at the 1%, 5%, and 10% levels, respectively.

Panel B in Table 4.3 displays the magnitude of the interaction effects of each latent factor and interbank competition on loan profitability. The authors' Hypothesis 2.4 predicted that using soft information limits lenders' losses despite interbank competition's negative effect on loan profitability. The subsequent regression analyses divided the HHI into three groups, and a dummy variable for high interbank competition was assigned to the bottom tercile group with a value of one if in the bottom tercile group, and zero otherwise, to create the interaction term between each of the soft information factor and high interbank competition.

The authors found that the coefficient of the interaction term between the networks or alliances/partnerships factor and high interbank competition is positive (0.0543), and significant at the 10% level (*t*-statistic: 1.95) in the full model. The coefficient of the interaction term between the business and leadership factor and high interbank competition is also positive (0.0631) and significant at the 5% level (*t*-statistic: 2.03). These results are consistent with the hypothesis. On average, interbank competition induces lenders' decreased profit, and the results suggest that using soft information, especially networks or alliances/partnerships and business and leadership information, enables lenders to offset the losses from severe interbank competition to a certain degree.

Further, the interaction term between the networks or alliances/partnerships factor and the high competition variable is more than twice the amount of the former factor's singular effect. It was also unanticipated that the interaction term between the business and management leadership factor and the high competition variable is more than six times the amount of the former factor's singular effect. The magnitudes of both factors in a competitive interbank environment are much greater than those in the full model, as Panel A in Table 4.3 illustrates. It is also noteworthy, especially in highlighting the interbank competitive environment, that a reversal occurs in the networks or alliances/partnerships factor's effects versus that of the business and management leadership factor. The interaction term between the business and management leadership factor and the high competition variable (0.0631) is 16% greater than the interaction term between the networks or alliances/partnerships factor and the high competition variable (0.0543). However, the interaction term between the networks or alliances/partnerships factor and the business and management leadership factor is not significant, as indicated by the interaction model displayed in Table 4.3, Panel A. This suggests that lenders hardly engage in both information production techniques at the same time, and management's philosophies and strategies completely determine whether to focus on centrally or peripherally located firm information. These results also suggest that these differential information production technologies require distinct competencies from loan officers for accessing, gathering, and processing such information.

4.3.2 Multivariate Analysis of the Bad Loan Ratio

The third to sixth columns from Panel A in Table 4.4 illustrate the results of the three latent factors' influence on bad loan ratios. The authors' Hypothesis 2.5 predicted negative coefficients for the three soft information factors—organizational systems, networks or alliances/partnerships, and business and leadership—with bad loan ratios. However, the authors' predictions were not supported by all three factors in the multivariate analysis, although data trends can be said to be consistent with the hypothesis. Analyses of the interaction models also provide similar results, as can be observed in the seventh to ninths columns from Panel A in Table 4.4.

The authors' Hypothesis 2.6 predicted a higher non-performing loan ratio when the lenders face severe interbank competition, or subsequently, a low HHI. The HHI's coefficients are significantly positive at 34.4802 (t-statistic: 2.73) at the 1% significance level, which is conveyed in the full model, illustrated in the sixth column from Panel A in Table 4.4, contrary to the hypothesis.

Multivariate analyses to test interbank competition's influence on bad loan ratios, further include the square terms of the HHI in the models to examine a lender's behavior toward risk under interbank competition, or the traditional "competition-fragility" perspective versus the modern "competition-stability" perspective (Berger et al. 2009).[3] The sixth column from Panel A in Table 4.6 displays the full model to reveal a negative coefficient of the HHI's square terms, at −78.8006 (t-statistic: −2.26) at the 5% significance level. This result indicates that the relationship between the HHI and a bad loan ratio follows an inverse U-shaped pattern (convex function), which initially rises, peaks, then declines. The authors present this inverse U-shaped relationship in Appendix 4.2, which is obtained from the regression model displayed in the sixth column in Panel A of Table 4.4 and adjusted for covariation with other control variables. The curve in the inverse U-shaped pattern peaks when the HHI is approximately 0.218. This curve suggests that lenders tend to lower their creditworthiness threshold as interbank competition becomes less severe, resulting in high bad loan ratios when they are located in the local area with an HHI less than 0.218, consistent with the competition-stability perspective. The modern competition-stability perspective suggests that monopoly power provokes banking instability, resulting in the assumption of risk.

Alternatively, this curve suggests that lenders tend to assume more credit risk as they confront increasing competition, resulting in high bad loan ratios, when they are located in local areas with HHIs greater than 0.218, consistent with the competition-fragility perspective. The traditional competition-fragility perspective suggests that interbank competition reduces their franchise value and exacerbates moral hazards, and therefore, they assume more credit risk.

Panel B in Table 4.4 displays the magnitudes of each latent factor and interbank competition's interaction effects on bad loan ratios. a dummy variable for high interbank competition was assigned to the bottom tercile group with a value of one if in the

---

[3]Section 2.4 provides definitions of the traditional "competition-fragility" and modern "competition-stability" perspectives.

Table 4.4 The effects of soft information and interbank competition on bad loan ratios

Panel A: Baseline model and interaction model—bad loan ratio								
Variables	Control variables	Single model			Full model	Interaction model		
	Coefficient (*t*-statistics)	Coefficient (*t*-statistics)			Coefficient (*t*-statistics)	Coefficient (*t*-statistics)		
Organizational systems (a)		−0.2444 (−1.37)			−0.2381 (−1.34)	−0.2532 (−1.38)	−0.2405 (−1.35)	−0.2383 (−1.34)
Networks (b)			−0.1643 (−0.96)		−0.1548 (−0.90)	−0.1423 (−0.80)	−0.1556 (−0.91)	−0.1557 (−0.90)
Business and leadership (c)				−0.0006 (−0.00)	0.0265 (0.16)	0.0187 (0.11)	0.0275 (0.16)	0.0264 (0.15)
Organ. systems × Networks						0.1249 (0.61)		
Organ. systems × Bus. and leader.							0.0105 (0.06)	
Networks × Bus. and leader.								0.0039 (0.02)
	***F*-statistics: (a) = (b) = (c) = 0**				***0.80***	***0.65***	***0.61***	***0.60***
Herfindahl	34.8551*** (2.77)	35.2828*** (2.81)	33.8476*** (2.68)	34.8514*** (2.76)	34.4802*** (2.73)	35.1270*** (2.76)	34.4628*** (2.72)	34.4522*** (2.72)
$Herfindahl^2$	−81.5189** (−2.34)	−81.2500** (−2.35)	−78.5182** (−2.25)	−81.5100** (−2.33)	−78.8006** (−2.26)	−80.6281** (−2.30)	−78.7665** (−2.26)	−78.7217** (−2.25)

(continued)

Table 4.4 (continued)

Panel A: Baseline model and interaction model—bad loan ratio								
Variables	Control variables	Single model			Full model	Interaction model		
	Coefficient (t-statistics)	Coefficient (t-statistics)			Coefficient (t-statistics)	Coefficient (t-statistics)		
Log (bank size)	0.2340 (0.81)	0.2117 (0.72)	0.2488 (0.86)	0.2340 (0.81)	0.2251 (0.77)	0.2214 (0.75)	0.2262 (0.77)	0.2248 (0.76)
Growth	−0.1692** (−2.12)	−0.1655** (−2.07)	−0.1672** (−2.09)	−0.1692** (−2.12)	−0.1641** (−2.05)	−0.1643** (−2.04)	−0.1640** (−2.04)	−0.1640** (−2.05)
(Growth − Ave. growth)^2	0.0040** (2.53)	0.0040** (2.51)	0.0040** (2.47)	0.0040** (2.53)	0.0039** (2.46)	0.0039** (2.45)	0.0039** (2.45)	0.0039** (2.45)
Branch ratio	3.1659*** (3.84)	3.1735*** (3.84)	3.1775*** (3.83)	3.1658*** (3.81)	3.1915*** (3.81)	3.1884*** (3.78)	3.1928*** (3.80)	3.1892*** (3.72)
SME lending ratio	0.0887*** (3.87)	0.0900*** (3.90)	0.0889*** (3.88)	0.0887*** (3.87)	0.0898*** (3.90)	0.0887*** (3.81)	0.0898*** (3.88)	0.0898*** (3.89)
Local share	0.0043 (0.18)	0.0063 (0.26)	0.0042 (0.17)	0.0043 (0.18)	0.0061 (0.25)	0.0052 (0.21)	0.0060 (0.24)	0.0060 (0.24)
Soft collecting (D)	−0.1278 (−0.41)	−0.1127 (−0.36)	−0.1162 (−0.37)	−0.1277 (−0.40)	−0.1071 (−0.33)	−0.1032 (−0.32)	−0.1082 (−0.33)	−0.1076 (−0.33)
Shinkin (D)	2.3998*** (4.76)	2.4131*** (4.76)	2.3526*** (4.56)	2.3998*** (4.75)	2.3679*** (4.57)	2.3663*** (4.59)	2.3696*** (4.56)	2.3675*** (4.56)
Mergers and HC (D)	0.3670 (0.69)	0.3424 (0.65)	0.3628 (0.68)	0.3670 (0.69)	0.3406 (0.65)	0.3440 (0.66)	0.3383 (0.65)	0.3404 (0.65)
Land price	−0.0664* (−1.88)	−0.0661 (−1.88)	−0.0700* (−1.94)	−0.0665* (−1.86)	−0.0689* (−1.92)	−0.0684* (−1.90)	−0.0691* (−1.91)	−0.0689* (−1.91)

(continued)

Table 4.4 (continued)

Panel A: Baseline model and interaction model—bad loan ratio

Variables	Control variables	Single model			Full model	Interaction model		
	Coefficient (t-statistics)	Coefficient (t-statistics)			Coefficient (t-statistics)	Coefficient (t-statistics)		
Job offers	0.9294* (1.88)	0.9786* (1.95)	0.9366* (1.88)	0.9294* (1.88)	0.9838* (1.95)	0.9542* (1.89)	0.9839* (1.94)	0.9825* (1.92)
Log (number of firms)	0.1976 (0.64)	0.2186 (0.70)	0.2020 (0.64)	0.1975 (0.64)	0.2245 (0.71)	0.2233 (0.71)	0.2243 (0.71)	0.2242 (0.71)
Urban (D)	−0.2058 (−0.48)	−0.1741 (−0.39)	−0.1638 (−0.37)	−0.2058 (−0.48)	−0.1382 (−0.31)	−0.1101 (−0.25)	−0.1356 (−0.30)	−0.1389 (−0.31)
Const.	−14.0802*** (−2.79)	−14.3039*** (−2.82)	−14.2519*** (−2.81)	−14.0802*** (−2.78)	−14.4601*** (−2.84)	−14.3191*** (−2.81)	−14.4650*** (−2.84)	−14.4490*** (−2.81)
No. of observations	307	307	307	307	307	307	307	307
R-Square	0.471	0.475	0.472	0.471	0.477	0.477	0.477	0.477

Panel B: Joint effects of soft information and competition—bad loan ratio

Variables	Control variables	Single model			Full model
	Coefficient (t-statistics)	Coefficient (t-statistics)			Coefficient (t-statistics)
Organizational systems (a)		−0.3377 (−1.34)			−0.3267 (−1.29)
Organ. systems × high comp (a)′		0.2422 (0.72)			0.2384 (0.70)

(continued)

Table 4.4 (continued)

Panel B: Joint effects of soft information and competition—bad loan ratio					
Variables	Control variables	Single model			Full model
	Coefficient (t-statistics)	Coefficient (t-statistics)			Coefficient (t-statistics)
***F*-statistics: (a) = (a)′ = 0**		***1.01***			***0.93***
Networks (b)			−0.323 (−1.42)		−0.3119 (−1.33)
Networks × high comp (b)′			0.442 (1.30)		0.4334 (1.25)
***F*-statistics: (b) = (b)′ = 0**			***1.11***		***0.99***
Business and leadership (c)				−0.0568 (−0.24)	0.0394 (0.16)
Bus. and leader. × high comp (c)′				0.1505 (0.48)	0.0461 (0.14)
***F*-statistics: (c) = (c)′ = 0**				***0.13***	***0.09***
	***F*-statistics: (a) = (b) = (c) = 0**				***1.04***
	***F* -statistics: (a)′ = (b)′ = (c)′ = 0**				***0.66***
Herfindahl	34.8551*** (2.77)	34.3819*** (2.73)	33.8665*** (2.69)	35.0636*** (2.75)	33.8436*** (2.66)
Herfindahl^2	−81.5189** (−2.34)	−78.3693** (−2.27)	−78.7097** (−2.26)	−82.2844** (−2.34)	−76.7958** (−2.18)
Log (Bank size)	0.2340 (0.81)	0.2207 (0.74)	0.2303 (0.79)	0.2157 (0.73)	0.2094 (0.69)

(continued)

Table 4.4 (continued)

Panel B: Joint effects of soft information and competition—bad loan ratio					
Variables	Control variables	Single model			Full model
	Coefficient (t-statistics)	Coefficient (t-statistics)			Coefficient (t-statistics)
Growth	−0.1692 (−2.12)	−0.1640 (−2.04)	−0.1701 (−2.11)	−0.1703 (−2.12)	−0.1663 (−2.04)
(Growth − Ave. growth)^2	0.0040** (2.53)	0.0040** (2.50)	0.0040** (2.46)	0.0040** (2.53)	0.0039** (2.43)
Branch ratio	3.1659*** (3.84)	3.2012*** (3.83)	3.1560*** (3.77)	3.1501*** (3.78)	3.2009*** (3.75)
SME lending ratio	0.0887*** (3.87)	0.0896*** (3.86)	0.0899*** (3.88)	0.0896*** (3.89)	0.0904*** (3.83)
Local share	0.0043 (0.18)	0.0066 (0.27)	0.0081 (0.33)	0.0064 (0.26)	0.0108 (0.42)
Soft collecting (D)	−0.1278 (−0.41)	−0.1323 (−0.41)	−0.1153 (−0.36)	−0.1316 (−0.41)	−0.1325 (−0.41)
Shinkin (D)	2.3998*** (4.76)	2.4293*** (4.83)	2.3600*** (4.55)	2.4035*** (4.76)	2.3914*** (4.61)
Mergers and HC (D)	0.3670 (0.69)	0.3171 (0.59)	0.3698 (0.70)	0.3823 (0.71)	0.3292 (0.62)
Land price	−0.0664* (−1.88)	−0.0671* (−1.89)	−0.0699* (−1.94)	−0.0660* (−1.85)	−0.0692* (−1.90)
Job offers	0.9294* (1.88)	0.9690* (1.95)	0.9367* (1.88)	0.9274* (1.88)	0.9730* (1.93)

(continued)

Table 4.4 (continued)

Panel B: Joint effects of soft information and competition—bad loan ratio					
Variables	Control variables	Single model			Full model
	Coefficient (*t*-statistics)	Coefficient (*t*-statistics)			Coefficient (*t*-statistics)
Log (number of firms)	0.1976 (0.64)	0.2239 (0.72)	0.2394 (0.75)	0.2026 (0.65)	0.2702 (0.84)
Urban (D)	−0.2058 (−0.48)	−0.1810 (−0.41)	−0.3435 (−0.73)	−0.2242 (−0.51)	−0.3305 (−0.68)
Const.	−14.0802*** (−2.79)	−14.4028*** (−2.83)	−14.4876*** (−2.86)	−13.9881*** (−2.76)	−14.7587*** (−2.90)
No. of observations	307	307	307	307	307
R-Square	0.471	0.476	0.475	0.471	0.480

Notes Table 4.1 provides definitions of the dependent and independent variables. ***, **, and * denote statistical significance at the 1%, 5%, and 10% levels, respectively.

bottom tercile group, and zero otherwise, to create the interaction term between each of the soft information factor and high interbank competition. The authors' Hypothesis 2.7 predicted that using soft information decreases bad loan ratios, although interbank competition has a negative effect. However, the authors' predictions were not supported by all three interaction terms between the high competition dummy and each latent factor.

4.4 Robustness Tests

This section empirically conducts robustness tests to assess the validity of this chapter's cross-sectional multivariate models. First, the authors conduct an *F*-test to ascertain whether a group of soft information factors significantly affects the dependent variable. Second, the authors assess each of the estimated factor scores' validity by using raw values for each questionnaire item. Third, the authors perform a random effects analysis to verify that estimates of the cross-sectional multivariate models' parameters do not vary among individuals or over time.

4.4.1 F-Test

The *F*-test confirms whether a group of variables' significance is useful. Here, the null hypothesis is that a set of variables has no effect on the dependent variable (Wooldridge 2015). First, regarding the models with a dependent variable of loan profitability, Panel A in Table 4.3 illustrates the null hypothesis' results, in that a set of soft information factor variables has no effect on a lender's performance. The null hypotheses were rejected in all four models at the 1% significance level, in the full model as well as the three interaction models (see the sixth to ninth columns at the ninth row). The *F*-tests confirm that both the baseline and interaction models fit the data better than the models with no soft information factor variables.

Second, each latent factor in the joint effects models interacted with a dummy variable for interbank competition. The results of the null hypothesis—that the model with no respective interaction term for each latent factor and a dummy variable for interbank competition[4] has no effect on lender performance—was rejected in two interaction terms—networks or alliances/partnerships and a dummy variable for interbank competition, and the business and management leadership and a dummy variable for interbank competition—at the 1% and 5% significance levels, respectively, as noted in the 8th and 11th rows at the last column in Panel B of Table 4.3.

---

[4]The authors divided the HHI into three groups, and a dummy variable with a value of one was assigned to the bottom tercile group, or high interbank competition (the dummy variable equals one if in the bottom tercile group, and zero otherwise).

Additionally, Panel B in Table 4.3 reveals the results of the null hypothesis that the model—which does not include all three interaction terms for each latent factor and a dummy variable for interbank competition—has no effect on loan profitability was subsequently rejected at the 10% significance level (see the 13th row at the last column). The authors confirm that a group of soft information factors is both jointly and statistically significant, even in the face of interbank competition, to lenders' profitability.

However, regarding the models with bad loan ratios as their dependent variable, the null hypothesis—that a set of soft information factor variables has no effect on lender performance—was not rejected in the full model or three interaction models (see the sixth to ninth columns at the ninth row in Table 4.4, Panel A). Further, the null hypothesis—that the model with no respective interaction term for each latent factor and a dummy variable of interbank competition has no effect on a lender's performance—was not rejected in the joint effect models (see the 5th, 8th, and 11th rows from Panel B in Table 4.4). Finally, the null hypothesis that the model—which does not include all three interaction terms for each latent factor and a dummy variable for interbank competition—has no effect on a bad loan ratio was also not rejected in the joint effect models (see the intersection of the 13th row and last column from Panel B in Table 4.4). In the models with bad loan ratios as a dependent variable, a group of soft information factors is jointly insignificant, and this also holds true when a lender faces interbank competition, which often justifies omitting them from the models. The F-statistics for a group of soft information factors' joint significance in bad loan ratios were consistent with this chapter's results, and this can also be applied when a lender faces interbank competition.

4.4.2 Assessment of the Factor Scores' Validity

As the authors discussed in Sect. 3.3, the unrotated component matrix generally has substantial cross-loadings, and does not maximize each variable's loadings on one factor, as the unrotated component matrix does not have a completely clean set of factor loadings (Ichikawa and Konishi 1995). Hence, a rotation technique is applied to improve the interpretation. Section 3.3 applied a varimax rotation, but the factor scores' estimates might involve a well-known problem: purported "rotational indeterminacy"—the factor scores' estimates might change if another rotation technique is applied. This means that the estimated factor scores are not uniquely defined, therefore this subsection uses raw questionnaire answers to additionally test whether this rotational indeterminacy problem critically impacts the multiple regression models' results with loan profitability as a dependent variable.

Additional tests add each respective questionnaire item's raw value, measured on a Likert scale from one to five and that constitute each soft information factor, to the model with no latent factors and loan profitability as its dependent variable. Further, the authors added an arithmetic mean value of the questionnaire items that construct each soft information factor in that model. The results indicate that the coefficients of the arithmetic mean values for the networks or alliances/partnership and business and management leadership factors are positive at the 1% and 5% significance levels, respectively. This is consistent with individual profitability models that involve the networks or alliances/partnership and business and management leadership factors as explanatory variables. These are respectively displayed in the fourth and fifth columns from Panel A in Table 4.3 (see Table 4.5). Therefore, the authors conclude that the factor scores' estimates in the multivariate regression models exhibit robustness against a variety of rotation techniques.

4.4.3 Random Effects GLS Regressions

This subsection conducted random effects GLS regressions to demonstrate that the parameter estimates—for which a cross-sectional multivariate analysis was performed for a single year—do not vary among individuals or over time. When model parameters vary in this manner, a cross-sectional analysis will not identify true model parameters, and this will lead to inefficient parameter estimates due to heteroskedasticity (Bowen and Wiersema 1999). Therefore, this subsection assumes that the three latent soft factors are time-invariant during the sample periods, and conducted a random effects analysis with sample periods from 2004 through 2007.[5] This allows these individual-specific effects to be disentangled from other time-invariant, unobserved individual effects in the error term, as the random effects model's error term contains both time-invariant and -variant unobserved effects. The data set used here is pooled across firms and years for a resulting unbalanced panel data set of 1,227 firm-year observations, as not all firms provided data for all years.

The following random effects GLS regression model is used to evaluate the analytical quality of a single-year cross-sectional multivariate analysis performed in this chapter:

$$\text{performance}_{i,t} = \alpha + \mathbf{f}_i'\beta + \mathbf{x}_{i,t}'\gamma + \mathbf{z}_{i,t}'\varsigma + \eta_i + \varepsilon_{i,t}, \quad i = 1, \ldots, N \quad t = 2004, \ldots, 2007,$$

where i represents the individual bank, as the use of the data panel structure allows for individual effects. The model involves the following independent variables: the first term $\mathbf{f}_i$ represents the time-invariant latent soft factor; the second term $x_{i,t}$ represents the bank-specific control variable, which incorporates an individual bank's specific micro-characteristics; the third term $z_{i,t}$ represents the local market's specific variable, which reflects the regional macro-economic characteristics; the term η_i represents other time-invariant, unobserved individual effects, such as unobserved individual characteristics; and the last term $\varepsilon_{i,t}$ is a pure error term. Additionally, the authors include a fixed time effect as a year dummy. Time dummies incorporate

[5]The extended sample periods are followed by the action program's 2003 introduction in Japan. This program anticipated that small/medium-sized and regional financial institutions would evaluate companies' future cash flows using soft information, and thus, enhance and strengthen their credit risk assessment capabilities in the fiercely competitive lending market (see Sect. 1.1).

Table 4.5 Regression results: the influence of each respective questionnaire item, and an arithmetic mean value of the items that construct each soft information factor that impacts loan profitability

	Coefficient	Robust S.E.	R-Square	SMRJ categories
Organizational systems				
Personnel evaluation system	−0.0294	0.0191	0.68	Organizational foundation
Company-specific improvement reporting system/the number of improvements	−0.0088	0.0220	0.68	Organizational foundation
Incentive system	−0.0364**	0.0183	0.68	Employees
Enhancement level of corporate education	−0.0269	0.0192	0.68	Organizational foundation
IT system equipment	−0.0320	0.0180	0.68	Organizational foundation
Efficient labor-management relations	−0.0045	0.0179	0.68	Organizational foundation
Employee knowledge	0.0022	0.0186	0.68	Employees
Arithmetic mean (Organizational systems)	−0.0317	0.0250	0.68	
Networks or alliances/partnerships				
Supplier relationships	0.0547***	0.0199	0.69	Customers/suppliers
Customer relationships	0.0385**	0.0185	0.68	Customers/suppliers
Supplier status	0.0366*	0.0201	0.68	Customers/suppliers
Customer status	0.0393**	0.0199	0.68	Customers/suppliers
Managers' seniority	0.0715***	0.0203	0.69	Manager
Management with industrial experience	0.0389*	0.0207	0.68	Manager
Manager networks	0.0474	0.0238	0.69	Manager
Arithmetic mean (Networks or alliances/partnerships)	0.0858***	0.0257	0.69	
Business and management leadership				
Management capability	0.0286	0.0211	0.68	Manager
Business plan	0.0281	0.0210	0.68	Organizational foundation
Managers' personality traits	0.0128	0.0197	0.68	Manager
Advantage in the core business	0.0507**	0.0210	0.69	Business contents

(continued)

Table 4.5 (continued)

	Coefficient	Robust S.E.	R-Square	SMRJ categories
Management leadership	0.0187	0.0212	0.68	Manager
Management philosophy	0.0475**	0.0186	0.69	Organizational foundation
Technological superiority	0.0279	0.0230	0.68	Business contents
Managerial succession	0.0151	0.0206	0.68	Manager
Arithmetic mean (Business and management leadership)	0.0728**	0.0340	0.69	

Note The control variables described in Table 4.3 are included in all regression models. ***, **, and * correspond to statistical significance at the 1%, 5%, and 10% levels, respectively.

several effects, including changes in external circumstances, having an impact on individuals' lending behavior, and any trend effects in this lending behavior (Praag et al. 2003).

The results of the random effects GLS regressions for the baseline and interaction models are consistent with those in the OLS regressions (see Panel A in Table 4.6). Regarding the models with loan profitability as the dependent variable, the null hypotheses—that a set of soft information factor variables has no effect on lender performance—are rejected in the full and three interaction models at the 1% significance level by the χ^2 test (see the fifth to eighth columns at the ninth row in Table 4.6, Panel A).

Further, the results of the random effects GLS regressions for the joint effects models, in which each latent factor interacts with a dummy variable for interbank competition, are consistent with those from OLS regressions (see Panel B in Table 4.6). The results of the null hypothesis—in that the model with no respective interaction term for each latent factor and a dummy variable for interbank competition has no effect on lender performance—is rejected in two interaction terms: the networks or alliances/partnerships and a dummy variable for interbank competition, and the business and management leadership and a dummy variable for interbank competition. These were found to be rejected at the 1% and 5% significance levels, respectively, in the χ^2 test (see the 8th and 11th rows in Panel B of Table 4.6). Finally, the result of the null hypothesis—in that the model that does not include all three interaction terms for each latent factor and a dummy variable for interbank competition has no effect on loan profitability—is also rejected at the 5% significance level (see the 13th row in the 5th column).

Given these findings, the authors can confirm that the estimates of the multivariate analysis' parameters in this chapter are insensitive to the multiple regressions' exact specifications.

Table 4.6 The results of random effects GLS regressions

Panel A: Baseline and interaction models

Variables	Loan profitability							Bad loan ratio						
	Single model			Full model	Interaction model			Single model			Full model	Interaction model		
	Coefficient (z-statistics)			Coefficient (z-statistics)	Coefficient (z-statistics)			Coefficient (z-statistics)			Coefficient (z-statistics)	Coefficient (z-statistics)		
Organizational systems (a)	−0.0187 (−1.33)			−0.0213 (−1.54)	−0.0242* (−1.79)	−0.0257* (−1.81)	−0.0203 (−1.47)	−0.2531* (−1.66)			−0.2471 (−1.62)	−0.2840* (−1.83)	−0.2532 (−1.60)	−0.2533* (−1.66)
Networks (b)		0.0457*** (3.16)		0.0435*** (3.07)	0.0457*** (3.14)	0.0420*** (2.96)	0.0485*** (3.34)		−0.1453 (−0.89)		−0.1312 (−0.79)	−0.1026 (−0.61)	−0.1332 (−0.81)	−0.1633 (−0.96)
Business and leadership (c)			0.0306* (1.86)	0.0254 (1.57)	0.0237 (1.46)	0.0271 (1.67)	0.0255 (1.59)			−0.0458 (−0.27)	−0.0197 (−0.11)	−0.0410 (−0.24)	−0.0174 (−0.10)	−0.0209 (−0.12)
Organ. systems × Networks					0.0226 (1.40)							0.2948 (1.61)		
Organ. systems × Bus. and leader						0.0192 (1.27)							0.0277 (0.18)	
Networks × Bus. and leader							−0.0222 (−1.44)							0.1412 (0.85)
	χ^2 statistics: (a) = (b) = (c) = 0			13.87***	15.46***	15.15***	16.15***	χ^2 statistics: (a) = (b) = (c) = 0			3.38	5.40	3.40	4.24
Herfindahl	0.6225*** (2.54)	0.6115*** (2.53)	0.6233*** (2.57)	0.6523*** (2.70)	0.6501*** (2.69)	0.6521*** (2.70)	0.6585*** (2.73)	14.164 (1.56)	13.809 (1.52)	13.811 (1.52)	13.926 (1.53)	14.811 (1.63)	13.856 (1.52)	13.484 (1.48)
Herfindahl^2								−25.255 (−0.91)	−25.212 (−0.91)	−25.511 (−0.92)	−24.476 (−0.88)	−27.225 (−0.98)	−24.365 (−0.88)	−23.269 (−0.84)
No. of observations	1,227	1,227	1,227	1,227	1,227	1,227	1,227	1,227	1,227	1,227	1,227	1,227	1,227	1,227

(continued)

Table 4.6 (continued)

Panel A: Baseline and interaction models

Variables	Loan profitability							Bad loan ratio						
	Single model			Full model	Interaction model			Single model			Full model	Interaction model		
	Coefficient (z-statistics)			Coefficient (z-statistics)	Coefficient (z-statistics)			Coefficient (z-statistics)			Coefficient (z-statistics)	Coefficient (z-statistics)		
Wald test: χ^2 statistics	845.81***	831.67***	843.82***	849.31***	876.63***	853.45***	857.45***	542.93***	546.75***	549.63***	551.86***	561.07***	551.66***	561.37***

Panel B: The joint effects of soft information and competition

Variables	Loan profitability				Bad loan ratio			
	Single model			Full model	Single model			Full model
	Coefficient (z-statistics)			Coefficient (z-statistics)	Coefficient (z-statistics)			Coefficient (z-statistics)
Organizational systems (a)	−0.0164 (−1.16)			−0.0214 (−1.56)	−0.3605** (−2.07)			−0.3605** (−2.07)
Organ. systems × high comp (a)′	−0.0058 (−0.64)			0.0013 (0.14)	0.2660 (1.37)			0.2869 (1.47)
χ^2 statistics: (a) = (a)′ = 0	***2.03***			***2.44***	***4.46***			***4.55***
Networks (b)		0.0373** (2.40)		0.0373** (2.43)		−0.1730 (−0.87)		−0.1562 (−0.75)
Networks × high comp (b)′		0.0231* (1.81)		0.0199 (1.50)		0.0759 (0.31)		0.0832 (0.33)
χ^2 statistics: (b) = (b)′ = 0		***14.53******		***13.63******		***0.81***		***0.59***

(continued)

Table 4.6 (continued)

Panel B: The joint effects of soft information and competition

Variables	Loan profitability				Bad loan ratio			
	Single model			Full model	Single model			Full model
	Coefficient (z-statistics)			Coefficient (z-statistics)	Coefficient (z-statistics)			Coefficient (z-statistics)
Business and leadership (c)			0.0224 (1.34)	0.0186 (1.12)			−0.0855 (−0.43)	−0.0461 (−0.22)
Bus. and leader. × high comp (c)′			0.0220** (2.06)	0.0210* (1.88)			0.1063 (0.56)	0.1141 (0.57)
χ^2 statistics: (c) = (c)′ = 0			***7.65***	***6.45***			***0.34***	***0.34***
	χ^2 statistics: (a) = (b) = (c) = 0			***9.83****	**χ^2 statistics: (a) = (b) = (c) = 0**			***5.19***
	χ^2 statistics: (a)′ = (b)′ = (c)′ = 0			***8.00***	**χ^2 statistics: (a)′ = (b)′ = (c)′ = 0**			***2.46***
Herfindahl	0.6206** (2.53)	0.6118*** (2.55)	0.6296** (2.61)	0.6683** (2.80)	14.147 (1.56)	13.785 (1.52)	13.837 (1.52)	13.951 (1.54)
Herfindahl^2					−24.738 (−0.90)	−25.146 (−0.91)	−25.628 (−0.93)	−24.090 (−0.87)
No. of observations	1,227	1,227	1,227	1,227	1,227	1,227	1,227	1,227
Wald test: χ^2 *statistics*	847.61***	850.68***	852.92***	882.82***	545.16***	546.66***	551.21***	555.51***

Note Section 4.2 provides definitions of loan performance, soft information, and the HHI. ***, **, and * correspond to statistical significance at the 1%, 5%, and 10% levels, respectively.

4.5 Conclusions

This chapter empirically tested the hypotheses established in Chap. 2 using a single year to provide a cross-sectional multivariate analysis of soft information use toward lender performance, specifically in local competitive markets. First, this chapter analyzed the relationship between the financial metrics of lender performance and soft information factors. The three latent factors were included in the multivariate regression model based on a factor analysis in Chap. 3. The results revealed that two latent factors—networks or alliances/partnerships and business and management leadership—positively impacted loan profitability. Alternatively, the organizational systems factor negatively influenced loan profitability.

Second, the chapter analyzed how any combination of soft information factors contributed to lender performance. The results indicated that the interaction term between the organizational systems and business and management leadership factors is significantly positive, although the organizational systems factor's solitary effect was significantly negative. This suggests that the simultaneous use of the organizational systems and business and management leadership factors eliminates the negative effect of a singular use of the organizational systems factor, and reverts loan profitability to its original level.

Third, the relationship between loan performance and soft information factors in interbank competition was analyzed. The results revealed that the networks or alliances/partnerships and business and leadership factors limit lenders' losses, although interbank competition negatively affects loan profitability.

Finally, the chapter additionally tested the estimates of the parameters from a single-year cross-sectional multivariate analysis do not vary among individuals or over time. An additional test expanded the sample period to include 2004–2007, and conducted a panel data study to consider individual and/or time effects. The authors assumed that the three latent soft factors are time-invariant during the sample periods to conduct a random effects analysis, which disentangled these individual-specific effects from other time-invariant, unobserved effects in the error term. The authors confirmed that the estimation results for a panel data study are consistent with those for the cross-sectional OLS regressions from the year 2008.

Appendix 4.1: Interbank Competition and Loan Performance

The multivariable regressions illustrated in Panel A of Table 4.3 consistently report the HHI's positive effect on loan performance. In the full model, the HHI's coefficient is 1.2083 at the 1% significance level. Figure 4.1 illustrates the linear relationship between the HHI and loan profitability, which has been adjusted for any covariation with other control variables in the full model, as displayed in the aforementioned Panel A of Table 4.3.

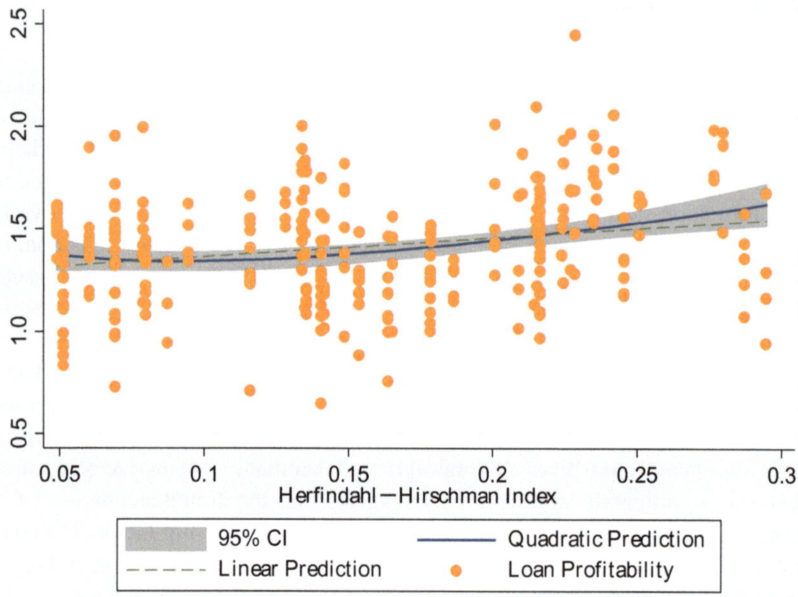

Fig. 4.1 The linear relationship between the HHI and loan profitability

Appendix 4.2: Interbank Competition and the Non-performing Loan Ratio

The multivariable regressions noted in Table 4.4, both Panel A and Panel B consistently report the HHI's square terms have a negative effect on bad loan ratios. The full model's HHI coefficient is -78.8006 at the 5% significance level, illustrated in the sixth column from Panel A in Table 4.4. Figure 4.2 depicts an inverse U-shaped relationship, obtained from the regression model displayed in the sixth column from Panel A in Table 4.4. The curve suggests that lenders tend to decrease their thresholds of creditworthiness as interbank competition becomes less severe, resulting in high bad loan ratios when they are located in the local area with an HHI less than 0.218, consistent with the competition-stability perspective. Alternatively, the curve suggests that lenders tend to assume more credit risk as they confront increasing competition, resulting in high bad loan ratios when they are located in the local area with HHIs greater than 0.218, which is consistent with the competition-fragility perspective.

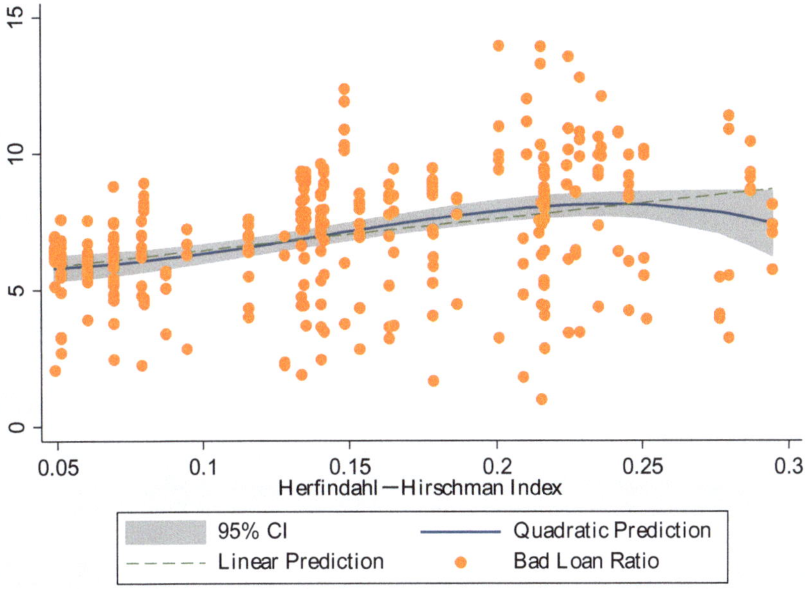

Fig. 4.2 The inverse U-shaped relationship between the HHI and bad loan ratio

References

Berger, A. N., De Young, R., & Udell, G. F. (2001). Efficiency barriers to the consolidation of the European financial services industry. *European Financial Management, 7*(1), 117–130.

Berger, A. N., Klapper, L. F., & Turk-Ariss, R. (2009). Bank competition and financial stability. *Journal of Financial Services Research, 35*(2), 99–118.

Berger, A. N., Miller, H., Petersen, M. A., Rajan, R. G., & Stein, J. C. (2005). Does function follow organizational form? Evidene from the lending practices of large and small banks. *Journal of Financial Economics, 76*(2), 237–269.

Bharath, S., Dahiya, S., Saunders, A., & Srinivasan, A. (2007). So what do I get? The bank's view of lending relationships. *Journal of Financial Economics, 85*(2), 368–419.

Bofondi, M., & Gobbi, G. (2006). Informational barriers to entry into credit markets. *Review of Finance, 10*(1), 39–67.

Bowen, H. P., & Wiersema, M. F. (1999). Matching method to paradigm in strategy research: Limitations of cross-sectional analysis and some methodological alternatives. *Strategic Management Journal, 20*(7), 625–636.

Carter, D. A., & McNulty, J. E. (2005). Deregulation, technological change, and the business-lending performance of large and small banks. *Journal of Banking & Finance, 29*(5), 1113–1130.

Carter, D. A., McNulty, J. E., & Verbrugge, J. A. (2004). Do small banks have an advantage in lending? An examination of risk-adjusted yields on business loans at large and small banks. *Journal of Financial Services Research, 25*(2–3), 233–252.

Castanias, R. P., & Helfat, C. E. (1991). Managerial resources and rents. *Journal of Management, 17*(1), 155–171.

Day, D. V., & Lord, R. G. (1988). Executive leadership and organizational performance: Suggestions for a new theory and methodology. *Journal of Management, 14*(3), 453–464.
Degryse, H., & Ongena, S. (2005). Distance, lending relationships, and competition. *The Journal of Finance, 60*(1), 231–266.
Degryse, H., & Ongena, S. (2007). The impact of competition on bank orientation. *Journal of Financial Intermediation, 16*(3), 399–424.
Gulati, R., Nohria, N., & Zaheer, A. (2000). Strategic networks. *Strategic Management Journal, 21*(3), 203–215.
Ichikawa, M., & Konishi, S. (1995). Application of the bootstrap methods in factor analysis. *Psychometrika, 60*(1), 77–93.
Inkpen, A. C., & Tsang, E. W. K. (2005). Social capital, networks, and knowledge transfer. *The Academy of Management Review, 30*(1), 146–165.
Jensen, M. C., & Meckling, W. H. (1996). Specific and general knowledge, and organizational structure. In P. S. Myers (Ed.), *Knowledge management and organizational design* (pp. 17–38). Boston: Butterworth-Heinemann.
Jimènez, G., & Saurina, J. (2004). Collateral, type of lender and relationship banking as determinants of credit risk. *Journal of Banking & Finance, 28*(9), 2191–2212.
Mamatzakis, E., Matousek, R., & Vu, A. N. (2016). What is the impact of bankrupt and restructured loans on Japanese bank efficiency? *Journal of Banking & Finance, 72,* S187–S202.
O'brien, R. M. (2007). A caution regarding rules of thumb for variance inflation factors. *Quality & Quantity, 41*(5), 673–690.
Podolny, J. M., & Page, K. L. (1998). Network forms of organization. *Annual Review of Sociology, 24*(1), 57–76.
Porter, M. E. (1991). Towards a dynamic theory of strategy. *Strategic Management Journal, 12*(S2), 95–117.
van Praag, B. M. S., Frijters, P., & Ferrer-i-Carbonellac, A. (2003). The anatomy of subjective well-being. *Journal of Economic Behavior & Organization, 51*(1), 29–49.
Radosevic, S. (1999). *International technology transfer and catch-up in economic development.* Cheltenham: Edward Elgar Publishing.
Stiroh, K. J., & Rumble, A. (2006). The dark side of diversification: The case of US financial holding companies. *Journal of Banking & Finance, 30*(8), 2131–2161.
Teece, D. J. (2000). Strategies for managing knowledge assets: The role of firm structure and industrial context. *Long Range Planning, 33*(1), 35–54.
Wooldridge, J. M. (2015). *Introductory econometrics: A modern approach* (6th ed.). Boston: Cengage Learning.

Chapter 5
Soft Information's Role in Lending Decisions

Abstract In this chapter, the authors interpret the empirical results from soft information usage's effects on lenders' decision making, especially concerning SMEs in regional banks as presented in Chap. 4. This chapter also interprets empirical evidence regarding interbank competition's influence on lender performance in the context of soft information usage. Soft information takes on abstract and elusive characteristics, and is considerably uncertain at the beginning of its collection. First, the results indicate that lenders encouraging intimate personal interactions that gather internally stored information—as exemplified by the firm's business plan and its managerial abilities to enforce and implement this plan within the firm—gain an enormous advantage in terms of profitability, specifically in interbank competition. Internally stored information is conceptualized as related to soft information in business and management leadership. As soft information knowledge spreads throughout local areas, it is easier for competitors and entrants to intervene in the extant lender–borrower relationship. Second, the empirical evidence illustrates that soft information from networks or appliances/partnerships generally leads to lenders' profitability, and further achieves a substantially greater effect in interbank competition compared to non-competitive markets.

Keywords Latent factor · Interbank competition · Business plan · Managerial leadership · Networks or alliances/partnerships · Industrial knowledge assets · Organizational systems · Organizational facades

5.1 Introduction

The authors test the hypotheses provided in Chap. 2 through univariate and multivariate analyses. In the former analysis, the authors compared the loan performance of lenders with high factor scores with those from lenders with low factor scores. In the latter analysis, the authors regress loan performance on soft information factors, the The Herfindahl-Hirschman index (HHI), and bank- and market-specific variables. Not all the results were consistent with the authors' expectations, and thus,

T. Yosano and T. Nakaoka, *Utilization of Soft Information on Bank Performance*, Development Bank of Japan Research Series,
https://doi.org/10.1007/978-981-13-8472-1_5

the authors primarily illustrate the results with a particular focus on these perverse results.

Additionally, much prior research has investigated univariate and multivariate relations between some proxy variables of soft information and loan performance, while they have yet to explore the association between the soft information component and loan performance. Hence, the authors further emphasize latent soft information variables, then discuss the analyses' results.

5.2 Soft Information's Effects on Loan Profitability

The authors' Hypothesis 2.1 predicted that lenders who collect and use soft information achieve higher lending performance in local lending markets. These results are consistent with the authors' prediction regarding soft information, particularly on both the networks or alliances/partnerships and business and management factors, although soft information on the organizational systems factor contradicts the authors' prediction. The univariate analysis' loan profitability from lenders with high factor scores for the networks or alliances/partnerships factor is greater than that of the lenders with low factor scores for the networks or alliances/partnerships factor. The loan profitability of lenders with high factor scores for the business and management leadership factor does not significantly differ from that of lenders with low factor scores for the business and management leadership factor; however, the loan profitability of lenders in a high tercile factor-score group for the business and management leadership factor is somewhat greater than that of lenders in low tercile factor-score group for the business and management leadership factor.

The authors also found the networks or alliances/partnerships factor positively and significantly affected loan profitability in the multivariate regression, both in the baseline and interaction models—regressions with latent variables' interaction effects. The results further indicated that the business and management leadership factor positively and significantly affects loan profitability in both the baseline and interaction models. Additionally, the slope coefficient of the networks or alliances/partnerships factor is 0.0413, and significant at the 1% level, which is greater than that of the business and management leadership factor, at 0.0299 in the baseline model. As the interaction model's results are almost the same as in the baseline model, this evidence suggests that lenders who use information from both the networks or alliances/partnerships factor and the business and management leadership factor in their lending decisions achieve high loan profitability, and the former has approximately 30% more of a critical effect than the latter.

Alternatively, the loan profitability of lenders with high factor scores for the organizational systems factor did not significantly differ from that of lenders with low factor scores on the organizational systems factor in the univariate analysis. The multivariate results further demonstrated negative, significant effects of the organizational systems factor on loan profitability in both the baseline and interaction models.

The interaction model further illustrated that the interaction term of the regression line between the organizational systems and business and management leadership factors is 0.0240, which is a positive effect. In considering the magnitude of the solitary organizational systems factor effect at −0.0274, simultaneously using information on business and management leadership eliminates the information's negative effect on the organizational systems and reverts loan profitability to its original level.

Additionally, Hypothesis 2.2 predicted that interbank competition decreases lenders' profit, while Hypothesis 2.3 stated that lenders in competitive local markets could acquire an informational advantage to limit their own losses through relationship lending. The results are compatible with the authors' predictions for both the networks or alliances/partnerships factor and the business and management leadership factor, although the organizational systems factor did not contribute to limiting the lender's decreased profitability in the face of interbank competition. The full interaction model's slope coefficients for the networks or alliances/partnerships factor and the interaction between the networks or alliances/partnerships factor and the dummy variable *High Comp*[1] are 0.0249 and 0.0543, respectively, which are positive and significant at the 10% level. The authors subsequently confirm that soft information on networks or alliances and partnerships achieves a substantially greater effect in interbank competition than the slope coefficient of the networks or alliances/partnerships factor, at 0.0413 in the baseline model. Moreover, the slope coefficient in the full interaction model of the interaction between the business and management leadership factor and the *High Comp* dummy variable is 0.0631, which is positive and significant at the 5% level, although that of the business and management leadership factor is not significant. The authors further confirm that soft information on business and management leadership contributes substantially to limit the lender's decrease in profitability due to interbank competition, although this might not be beneficial for lenders who do not face interbank competition. Finally, the slope coefficient of the interaction between the organizational systems factor and the *High Comp* dummy variable is not significant.

5.3 Soft Information's Role in Lending Decisions

The production of soft information—defined as unquantifiable, unverifiable, and sometimes subjective—is an essential part of relationship lending (Berger and Udell 2002). Gathering and processing soft information requires the expertise and labor of loan officers, as well as repetitive personal interactions, and subsequently, the intimate relationships with borrowers that this creates. This strengthens the lender–borrower relationship and enables lenders to gain specific knowledge of SMEs' businesses and judge their overall health. The core information on SMEs' businesses and their creditworthiness involves substantially abstract aspects of various business compo-

[1]*High Comp* takes a value of zero for "concentration" if the HHI is in the middle and highest terciles, and one for "competition" if the HHI is in the lowest tercile.

nents (characteristics), and thus poses difficulties innate to numeric measurement. Loan officers utilize their skills and expertise from within the field to acquire a certain caliber of soft information. This is gathered through personal interaction with borrowers, their suppliers and customers, and related parties in local industries. The loan officer must build on his or her experience in local industries, which requires that they not only store distinctive information on local industries, but also gain years of experience in such related fields as local sales or supply chain networks.

Figure 5.1 illustrates the soft information attributes and how they shift as time advances. Soft information takes on abstract and elusive characteristics, and is considerably uncertain at the beginning of such a collection. However, this becomes condensed as time passes and repetitive interactions take place, with lessening uncertainty. As soft information knowledge permeates the local area, it is easier for competitors and entrants to intervene in the extant lender–borrower relationship. Therefore, the sooner an incumbent lender builds information barriers, the higher the barriers become. This consequently helps insulate the incumbent lender from the threat of new entrants, although this involves enormous labor costs. In the late-middle stage, a large portion of this soft information has become common knowledge in local industries. However, even if it becomes known in the local industrial market, hardly any private and proprietary information is documented, and is therefore still not reflected in such data as bank references and trade references, which act as input data in the credit scoring model. In fact, a significant portion of information in the late-middle stage, such as advanced technological capabilities and products' or services' reliability, has become common knowledge among local industries. Alternatively, such information as innovative knowledge, research and development, and related technologies are protected and stored internally within the firm through strict information protection policies. The latter information is still not reflected in its products/services, although the reputation on the concerned information circulates within the local market through speculation and hearsay. The former information may become condensed and less uncertain, but the latter must be kept elusive and uncertain.

5.4 Three Latent Factors and Information Efficacy

5.4.1 Business and Management Leadership

This book categorizes three soft information factors based on survey data: organizational systems, networks or alliances/partnerships, and business and management leadership. The last factor consists of two subfactors: First, the business subfactor includes questionnaire items comprised of a business plan, any advantage in the core business, and technological superiority. Second, the management leadership subfactor is comprised of questionnaire items pertaining to management capabilities, managers' personality traits, management's leadership and philosophy, and man-

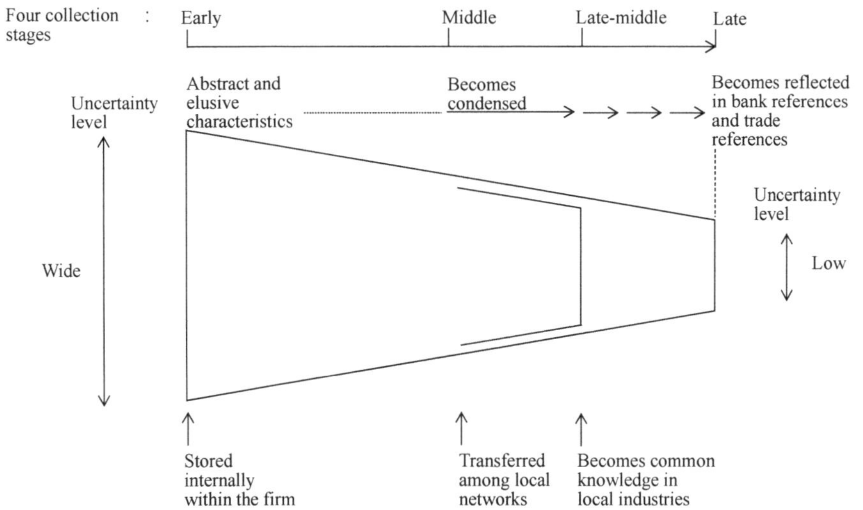

Fig. 5.1 Attributes of soft information and how they shift as time advances

agerial succession. This information is located at the heart of the firm, and thus is difficult to become known without intimate personal contact with integral members at the center of the firm. These are highly abstract, in-depth concepts.

Small businesses are informationally opaque as a result of their lack of track records; therefore, lenders must obtain their private and proprietary information to assess their businesses' stability and growth opportunities. Thus, constructing a business plan is essential and indispensable for small businesses to receive financing from lenders. It provides borrowers a chance to impress prospective financing sources and allows them to pitch their proposals to lenders. If practicable, lenders assess the business plan from the following four viewpoints (Rumelt 1988): (1) the plan's internal consistency, (2) external consonance, (3) the creation and/or maintenance of competitive advantage, and (4) the plan's feasibility.

First, lenders assess whether the company has developed and implemented an internally consistent set of objectives and functional policies that collectively define its market position (Porter 1991). Demand forecasting is a crucial element in the business plan, as it involves investigating the demand for the companies' products and services, which include the current and projected demand by industry and products' end users in the market. Competent demand forecasting enables firms to propose internally consistent plans equipped with well-timed, productive, and cost-effective business operations. Second, lenders analyze these business plans to ensure that they represent an adaptive response to both the external environment and the critical changes occurring within it (Rumelt 1988). Firms may also have to react to unexpected circumstances, and firms that face high turbulence must rely on substantial strategic planning to cope with changing, unpredictable conditions; firms facing low turbulence need less strategic planning (Miller and Cardinal 1994). Thus, lenders are motivated to evaluate the firm's level of turbulence the firm faces, then must further judge whether the firm has prepared an appropriate strategic plan and can anticipate, prepare for, and cope with disruptions in the target markets under highly turbulent conditions. Third, lenders identify the development and maintenance of relevant assets and skills, on which they base their selection of strategies and competitive arenas, such that those assets and skills form a sustainable competitive advantage (Aaker 1989). Fourth, lenders judge the business plan's feasibility, which involves the firm's ability to meet its financing and other resource requirements and accurately predict supplier prices and wage rates. Their relevant assets and skills are crucial resources when executing the business plan, as these provide operational superiority or may create a superior market position, which allows the firm to generate superior returns (Reed et al. 2000). Following the business plan's implementation, it is essential for the firm to mobilize its internal assets and skills toward the organization's strategic direction. Indicators conveying the strength of their assets and skills are thus required to measure performance and guide the programs needed to improve assets and skills (Aaker 1989). However, these contain several abstract concepts innate to numerical assessment that can consequently pose difficulties in their analysis.

Internal assets and skills are typified by the firm's core businesses and technologies, are rooted in the firm's routines, and are not easily transferred due to the gradual learning process (Radosevic 1999) and intrinsic characteristics of tacit knowledge. The workforce must assimilate these valuable internal assets and skills through the learning process (Wahab et al. 2012) and store these resources as tacit knowledge in the organization; these resources pose innate difficulties in their documentation.

The leadership and management experts who lead and direct the entire organization also develop, protect, and exploit internal resources and skills to promote the organization's business in line with its business plan. Enterprise management leadership underpins the business disciplines that require the workforce to mobilize internal resources in the appropriate direction. Further, managerial experts reach their maximum potential in implementing appropriate strategic plans when the firm faces high turbulence. The business' success entirely depends on its management's abilities, authority, and behaviors. It is solely the management team's responsibility to determine whether the firm properly utilizes or wastes internal resources and skills. Moreover, Day and Lord's (1988) analysis of previous studies suggests that top managerial leadership explains 20 to 45% of a firm's performance. This emphasizes the importance of managerial leadership in determining firms' performance. Castanias and Helfat (1991) identified three basic types of managerial skills: generic, industry-related, and firm-specific. Lenders judge managerial leadership as well as the coherence in the types of managerial skills within the firm's business operations to clarify whether the firm operates its business both effectively and efficiently.

The results reveal that the business and management leadership factor contributes to loan profitability when lenders face interbank competition, but does not function effectively in a highly concentrated market. Regarding loan profitability, lenders need not attempt to probe and delve deeper into its information while market competition is not so severe. Lenders could raise or mitigate downward trends in loan profitability by gathering in-depth information in the face of competition, although substantial effort and labor costs are required. If so, then this scenario is consistent with Hypothesis 2.3, which predicted local market competition motivates lenders to acquire an investment advantage through the collecting and processing of soft information.

Additionally, the authors predict a substitution effect exists in the face of interbank competition, which encourages lenders' shift away from transaction-based lending and toward relationship-based lending. Simultaneously, the authors also anticipate that lenders cannot devote significant efforts to each lending technology, and thus, each lending type becomes less value-added and profitable, in line with Hauswald and Marquez's (2006) work. However, this result appears to contradict the authors' prediction, in that the business and management leadership factor can function more effectively when accompanied by increased interbank competition. The magnitude of the coefficient of the interaction between the business and management leadership factor and the *High Comp* dummy variable is greatest among the three interaction terms with the *High Comp* dummy variable in the full interaction model—the interactions between the *High Comp* dummy variable and the organizational systems factor, the *High Comp* dummy variable and the networks or alliances/partnerships factor, and the *High Comp* dummy variable and the business and management leadership factor. Far from reducing informational investments in the business and management leadership factor, highly profitable lenders are instead motivated to probe deeper into firm information to be insulated from the threat of competitors and new entrants. The business and management leadership information is difficult to access, but gathering and processing such information might be more effective and better contribute to profitability when lenders face interbank competition; in contrast, no substantial time and effort should be spent in gathering and processing such information in the monopolistic market from the loan profitability perspective.

Japan's Financial Service Agency (FSA) aims at this result in its action program (FSA 2003) and subsequent Financial Monitoring Policy (FSA 2014). The action program requires small and medium-sized/regional financial institutions to shift from transaction-based to relationship lending. Moreover, the new Financial Monitoring Policy further initiated the monitoring of small and medium-sized/regional financial institutions to ensure steady SME lending based on business assessments. The business and management leadership factor is considered central in evaluating SMEs' businesses to survive tough market competition.

5.4.2 Networks or Alliances/Partnerships

The networks or alliances/partnerships factor consists of two subfactors: first, the network subfactor, the questionnaire items for which are comprised of the supplier and customer relationships, supplier status, and customer status. The second subfactor is industrial knowledge assets, which are comprised of such questionnaire items as managers' seniority, management with industrial experience, and managers' networks.

The network organization is defined as a collection of actors that pursue repeated, enduring exchange relationships with one another (Podolny and Page 1998). Tightly woven networks encompass a firm's set of horizontal and/or vertical relationships with other organizations, whether suppliers, customers, competitors, or other entities; this also includes relationships across industries. These networks are composed of enduring interorganizational ties that are of strategic significance for the firms entering them. Such networks include a wide range of forms: intercorporate business units, strategic alliances, buyer-supplier relationships, and trade associations, among others (Gulati et al. 2000; Inkpen and Tsang 2005). Lenders' competitive advantage is sourced by assets surrounding industrial knowledge, and this competitive advantage flows from the creation, ownership, protection, and use of difficult-to-imitate commercial and industrial assets; such assets include both technical and organizational tacit and codified knowledge (Teece 2000). Local industrial management networks are inherently close-knit, and work together to create and enhance commercial and industrial knowledge assets. Therefore, this relationship enables lenders to build and maintain prominent positions in their local markets.

The knowledge of the lender's interest is primarily and highly tacit, difficult to obtain, and stored internally in the firm. However, networks from the industrial district over time can learn and share their basic knowledge of their products and/or services among a group of geographically close firms (Helmsing 2001; Inkpen and Tsang 2005). Geographic proximity facilitates the distribution of knowledge and its exchange among local firms (Marshall 1920). Abstract knowledge concepts—such as the business model and technological superiorities, both of which are embedded in the firm's products and/or services—are gradually transferred within boundary organizations. The spatial movement of knowledge within the boundaries of an industrial district involves a variety of channels: the labor force's interfirm mobility within the district, alongside interactions between suppliers, customers, producers, and users of capital equipment (Keeble and Wilkinson 1999; Inkpen and Tsang 2005). This transference of knowledge enables industrial districts to store cumulative and local knowledge, which has evolved beyond the firm's boundaries (Inkpen and Tsang 2005). This provides lenders with an opportunity to obtain the firm's business and technical information by interacting with local industries.

Any private and proprietary information is hardly documented, such as bank and trade references; therefore, is not reflected in the data, but it is easier for lenders to access information from network and industry management experts than information stored internally within the firm—business and management leadership. The results support this illustration, as a notable feature of the networks or alliances/partnerships factor is that it even functions in non-competitive markets. The networks or alliances/partnerships factor functions even in monopolistic markets, but the business and management leadership factor does not work in a highly concentrated market. This suggests that highly profitable lenders typically gather and process these types of information in local industrial markets.

Additionally, the networks or alliances/partnerships factor functions simultaneously and more effectively in competitive markets. Essentially, the magnitude of the coefficient of the interaction between networks or alliances/partnerships and the *High*

Comp dummy variable is greater than that of the networks or alliances/partnerships variable alone. Lenders parallel business and management leadership through their intense motivation to search for relevant information in boundary organizations when faced with interbank competition. The authors conclude that lenders routinely gather information on networks or alliances/partnerships to build informational barriers, and are further motivated to probe deeper into information on business and management leadership to be insulated from the threat of competitors and new entrants when interbank competition occurs.

5.4.3 Organizational Systems

The organizational systems factor consists of three subfactors: first, a subfactor of the human resource management system, the questionnaire items for which are comprised of a personnel evaluation system, a company-specific improvement reporting system, and an incentive system. The second subfactor is the management system's effectiveness, the questionnaire items for which include the enhancement level for corporate education, employee knowledge, and efficienct labor–management relations. The third subfactor pertains to IT system equipment.

Organizational systems consider three critical performance factors: strategy, organization, and motivation (Myers 1996). Firms ensure the steady implementation of their business and strategic plan by introducing and renewing their organizational systems. This enables their organizations to perform better, learn accurately and promptly, and adapt appropriately to deal with changes in organizational needs and business conditions. Organizational systems also utilize the process and rules that govern not only the measures and performance used to evaluate employees' actions, but also the rewards and punishments imposed on those employees as a consequence of their own misdemeanor (Jensen and Meckling 1996). Ideally, firms will be dedicated to adhering to their employees' rights by utilizing their authoritative positions to its full potential and partitioning workers as best as they can. However, such a harmonious collocation of appropriate rights with particular positions within organizations is challenging in practice. Generally, it is impossible to structure, control, and encourage a system that will cause employees to behave exactly as managers wish. Additionally, control and incentive systems are costly to design and implement. Specifically, agency costs are the costs to design, implement, and maintain appropriate incentive and control systems (Jensen and Meckling 1996).

Organizational system information is easier to access through outside organizations than other categories of information, such as business and management leadership, and networks or alliances/partnerships. The organization's appearance as illustrated by its organizational systems may reflect its assertiveness, confidence, and managerial expertise. Further, organizational systems help create a sense of trust and reliability, and furthermore, achieve an appearance of certainty. Nevertheless, this could be an illusion, as managers could construct organizational façades—whether artificial in appearance or effect—to mislead external stakeholders. Organizational façades help managers justify their actions, acquire environmental sources, and gain direction. Moreover, managers may also need to appear competent to raise funds from sources external to their firms, and may also adopt fashionable structures simply to appear contemporary. Some are skeptical about whether they really attempt to improve these organizations (Nystrom and Starbuck 1984). As restructuring incentive and control systems incur enormous agency costs, whether fashionable organizational structures directly lead to stronger firm performance depends on how these systems are implemented. Even if the firm introduces new or renewed organizational structures to achieve more efficient control and incentive systems, the certain possibility still exists that this would harm the profitability resulting from substantial agency costs. Otherwise, if the firm introduces fashionable structures simply to compensate for aesthetics or the organization's appearance to appeal to outside stakeholders, this not only demonstrates a firm's lack of relationship with their organizational management and operations, but also possibly and adversely have a negative impact on performance.

The results revealed that organizational systems negatively and significantly affect loan profitability in the base line model. This suggests that if lenders heavily trust in the organization's superficial appearance, the organizational façade might mislead them, as those pieces of information are easily obtained.

The interaction term between the organizational systems and the business and management leadership factor is positive and significant, which suggests that the simultaneous use of the business and management leadership factor can offset the negative effect of the organizational systems factor's single use in the interaction model. Collecting business and management leadership information requires substantial, labor costs, but its effect nevertheless accomplishes little more than ensuring loan profitability returns to normal, original levels, when lenders use organizational systems information. The negative consequences from a heavy reliance on the organizational façade are extensive, with one insight revealing that a negative effect of the organizational systems factor is the wasted effort in gathering and processing information on business and management leadership.

In the later stage of the information collection process, and as time progresses, a substantial portion of firms' businesses, their potential growth, and their financial stability are reflected in their bank and trade references. A bank reference contains information about the firm's history and relationship with its financial institution. Such references represent the firm's financial condition and stability, and its ability to maintain sound relationships with financial institutions. A trade reference also involves an exchange of firms' goods and/or services, typically between businesses; includes payments for parts, supplies, and materials; and might also involve advertising and other services. In this stage, it is easier for external competitors to intervene in the incumbent lender–borrower relationship and offer loan contracts to the borrower; consequently, the borrower's departure becomes increasingly possible.

5.5 Concluding Remarks

This book has examined the influence of using soft information in relationship lending on lenders' loan profitability and their ability to determine borrowers' creditworthiness, with a particular focus on interbank competition in local credit markets. Therefore, this book constructs its sample using regional, second-tier regional, and shinkin banks. As soft information is difficult to quantify, verify, and document, it is consequently protected, and its access is controlled to a considerable extent to deter borrowers from competitors and entrants. Almost all previous research has investigated the relationship between using soft information and loan performance with proxies of soft information utilization, including: duration, or the period of time since a lender granted its first loan to a borrower; scope, or the breadth of the relationship as measured by the number of different financial products or services a borrower receives from a lender; and the borrower-lender distance, or the physical distance from the lending office to a borrower. Previous research used proxies for the use of soft information due to the difficulties inherent in numerically measuring soft information. This study is one of the first to use questionnaire survey data from lender representatives in a factor analysis to identify the underlying factors of soft information that benefit lenders. Further, this work analyzes the relationship between the financial metrics of lender performance and soft information factors in interbank competition; it also provides empirical results that demonstrate the use of soft information allows lenders to attain more precise lending decisions.

This book categorizes three soft information factors: organizational systems, networks or alliances/partnerships, and business and management leadership. The organizational systems factor involves the process and rules that govern not only the measures and performance used to evaluate employees' actions, but also the rewards and punishments imposed on those employees as a consequence of their misdemeanor (Jensen and Meckling 1996). This appears to be related to the organization's appearance, and is characterized by easier accessibility than other factors. The networks or alliances/partnerships factor represents boundaries, external networks, and industrial knowledge assets, all of which can be gathered in areas peripheral to clients' businesses. As its name implies, the business and management leadership factor is located at the heart of the firm. This factor involves the firm's business plan, internal assets and skills, and ability to lead or direct the entire organization. This factor is difficult to access, as lenders are cannot reach out for in-depth information from integral members in the center of the firm due to the lack of intimate personal contact.

The authors' findings demonstrate that the production of information—especially on business and management leadership and network and business/leadership factors—plays an essential role in promoting a bank's profitability. Additionally, the authors found that these effects are strong even when banks face high interbank competition. Far from reducing informational investments regarding business and management leadership, which would result in lower loan profitability, greater interbank competition encourages lenders to secure this in-depth information to insulate them from the threat of new entrants. Further unearthed information on business and management leadership contributes to a lender's profitability, even under harsher interbank competition.

This book's results support the objectives of Japan's FSA, as the action program encourages small and medium-sized/regional financial institutions to shift from transaction-based to relationship lending. The FSA's new Financial Monitoring Policy further promotes small and medium-sized/regional financial institutions' SME lending steadily based on business assessments through its monitoring program. The centrally located information on business and management leadership and peripherally located information on networks or alliances/partnerships are sources of business opportunities from soft information-based lending, which lenders can use to judge SMEs' businesses. Therefore, gathering these two types of information not only improves bankers' lending profitability, but it also fosters and enhances their community knowledge and enables them to survive in an intensive competitive market.

This book further surprisingly supports the notion that lenders' excessive reliance on the organizational systems factor hinders loan profitability. Information that typifies the organization's appearance—or the façade that the firm uses to advocate their assertiveness, confidence, and management expertise through its organizational systems—can possibly have a negative influence on banks' lending profitability. This negative effect is caused by the singular use of organizational systems' information, and persists until lenders can obtain in-depth, central information on firms' business and management leadership. Using information on business and management leadership in parallel with the organizational systems offsets the negative effect of a façade of assertiveness.

This book's results suggest that two types of profitable business models exist in which relationship banks gather information on their borrowers. The first type emphasizes intimate personal interactions, and the loan officer contacts integral members in the center of the firm to gather such in-depth information as the firm's businesses and management leadership. The second focuses more on collecting information in the local industrial market, and identifies the information-collecting method as contacting relevant acquaintances, or those with specific knowledge of the local industrial market. The loan officer builds his or her experience by becoming a constituent member in the local market, establishing a sense of mutual understanding, and strengthening solidarity among regional market constituents. Both business models are suitable and can be used to attain more precise lending decisions.

References

Aaker, D. A. (1989). Managing assets and skills: The key to a sustainable competitive advantage. *California Management Review, 31*(2), 91–106.

Berger, A. N., & Udell, G. F. (2002). Small business credit availability and relationship lending: The importance of bank organisational structure. *The Economic Journal, 112*(477), 32–53.

Castanias, R. P., & Helfat, C. E. (1991). Managerial resources and rents. *Journal of Management, 17*(1), 155–171.

Day, D. V., & Lord, R. G. (1988). Executive leadership and organizational performance: Suggestions for a new theory and methodology. *Journal of Management, 14*(3), 453–464.
FSA (2003). *Action program concerning enhancement of relationship banking function*. Financial Services Agency. Retrieved from http://www.fsa.go.jp/news/newse/e20030328-1a.pdf.
FSA (2014). *Financial monitoring policy for 2014–2015 (Policy for supervision and inspection)*. Financial Services Agency. Retrieved from http://www.fsa.go.jp/en/news/2014/20141225-1/01.pdf.
Gulati, R., Nohria, N., & Zaheer, A. (2000). Strategic networks. *Strategic Management Journal, 21*(3), 203–215.
Hauswald, R., & Marquez, R. (2006). Competition and strategic information acquisition in credit markets. *The Review of Financial Studies, 19*(3), 967–1000.
Helmsing, B. (2001). Externalities, learning and governance: New perspectives on local economic development. *Development and Change, 32*(2), 277–308.
Inkpen, A. C., & Tsang, E. W. K. (2005). Social capital, networks, and knowledge transfer. *The Academy of Management Review, 30*(1), 146–165.
Jensen, M. C., & Meckling, W. H. (1996). Specific and general knowledge, and organizational structure. In P. S. Myers (Ed.), *Knowledge management and organizational design* (pp. 17–38). Boston: Butterworth-Heinemann.
Keeble, D., & Wilkinson, F. (1999). Collective learning and knowledge development in the evolution of regional clusters of high technology SMEs in Europe. *Regional Studies, 33*(4), 295–303.
Marshall, A. (1920). *Principles of Economics* (8th ed.). UK: Palgrave Macmillan.
Miller, C. C., & Cardinal, L. B. (1994). Strategic planning and firm performance: A synthesis of more than two decades of research. *The Academy of Management Journal, 37*(6), 1649–1665.
Myers, P. S. (1996). Knowledge management and organizational design: An introduction. In P. S. Myers (Ed.), *Knowledge management and organizational design* (pp. 1–6). Boston: Butterworth-Heinemann.
Nystrom, P. C., & Starbuck, W. H. (1984). Organizational facades. *Academy of Management Proceedings, 1984*(1), 182–185.
Podolny, J. M., & Page, K. L. (1998). Network forms of organization. *Annual Review of Sociology, 24*(1), 57–76.
Porter, M. E. (1991). Towards a dynamic theory of strategy. *Strategic Management Journal, 12*(S2), 95–117.
Radosevic, S. (1999). *International technology transfer and catch-up in economic development*. Cheltenham: Edward Elgar Publishing.
Reed, R., Lemak, D. J., & Mero, N. P. (2000). Total quality management and sustainable competitive advantage. *Journal of Quality Management, 5*(1), 5–26.
Rumelt, R. P. (1988). Evaluating business strategy. In J. B. Quinn, H. Mintzberg, & R. M. James (Eds.), *The strategy process: Concepts, and cases*. New Jersey: Englewood Cliffs.
Teece, D. J. (2000). Strategies for managing knowledge assets: The role of firm structure and industrial context. *Long Range Planning, 33*(1), 35–54.
Wahab, S. A., Rose, R. C., & Wati Osman, S. I. (2012). Defining the concepts of technology and technology transfer: A literature analysis. *International Business Research, 5*(1), 61–71.

Index

T. Yosano and T. Nakaoka, *Utilization of Soft Information on Bank Performance*, Development Bank of Japan Research Series,
https://doi.org/10.1007/978-981-13-8472-1

MIX
Papier aus verantwortungsvollen Quellen
Paper from responsible sources
FSC® C105338

If you have any concerns about our products,
you can contact us on
ProductSafety@springernature.com

In case Publisher is established outside the EU,
the EU authorized representative is:
Springer Nature Customer Service Center GmbH
Europaplatz 3, 69115 Heidelberg, Germany

Printed by Libri Plureos GmbH
in Hamburg, Germany